TIGER

TIGER
A HOCKEY STORY

TIGER WILLIAMS
WITH
JAMES LAWTON

Douglas & McIntyre
Vancouver/Toronto

4th printing, 1984

Douglas & McIntyre Ltd., 1615 Venables Street,
Vancouver, British Columbia V5L 2H1

Canadian Cataloguing in Publication Data

Lawton, James.
  Tiger

ISBN 0–88894–448–9

1. Williams, Tiger, 1954–   2. Hockey players –
Canada – Biography.   I. Title.
GV848.5.W54L39 1984   796.96′2′0924   C84–091225–0

Cover photograph by James La Bonté
Design by Barbara Hodgson
Printed and bound in Canada by D. W. Friesen & Sons

For Brenda,
who made me understand there was life outside hockey,
and for the game,
which has so enriched that life.

Acknowledgements

So many people have helped me in my career and in realizing my ambition to one day sit down and put it all on paper. Hockey fans have been a great encouragement to me, and I hope that they will feel that in this book I have given them some accounting, some explanations and some feeling of what it is like being a pro. For doing so much to make the book happen I am grateful to my friends Bill McIntosh, agent and Bruce McColl, lawyer. James Lawton wishes to join me in appreciation of the skilled and patient editing of Lyall Campbell.

David "Tiger" Williams

1

He had been known as Tiger from his first day on the frozen river at Weyburn, Saskatchewan. Then, he was five years old, ungainly in his ill-fitting skates and wielding an outsized hockey stick but also magnetic in the way he tried to impose himself upon the action. Now, nearly twenty years later, he gave little hint of why he should have such a ferocious reputation as he sat in Number One courtroom of the justice building on University Avenue in Toronto. He wore an expensively cut suit, the kind you rarely see in Weyburn, and a neutral expression. Occasionally, David Williams would make a note, lean forward to whisper to his lawyer, Tom Forbes; from time to time, he would raise his eyebrows in reaction to some point made by the prosecution and then he would shake his head, but not ostentatiously.

Forbes, a leading trial lawyer, would say later that he had been astonished by the self control of a young man already well on his way to becoming the most penalized player in the long and notably violent history of Canada's national game. The lawyer detected two great qualities in the hockey player. He noted an extraordinary single-mindedness, and absolute conviction about who he was and what he was doing. He also saw a striking talent for quickly assessing a situation and making an appropriate response. In the courtroom, this required the hockey player to keep a tight rein on his emotions. For the truth was plain enough to Tom Forbes, who had much experience of watching men from all walks of life undergo fierce pressure. Forbes knew that during more than a month of almost daily court appearances in the fall of 1977 David Williams was in a state of permanent rage. To conceal this rage he wore an amiable mask which had not slipped once, at least not in the courtroom. Forbes, however, did not wish to push his luck. He decided against putting Williams in the witness box.

Williams was before an Ontario provincial judge, the Honourable Hugh Locke, on charges brought by Attorney General Roy McMurtry. It was said that on the occasion of a National Hockey League game between the Toronto Maple Leafs and the Pittsburgh Penguins, Williams had in his possession an offensive weapon, a hockey stick, and that he did assault Dennis Owchar, a Pittsburgh player who required forty-six stitches in a head wound.

Forbes spent weeks jockeying with the crown prosecutors led by Bob McGee. There was some talk of plea bargaining, but Forbes knew that the hockey player would have dismissed the idea with some contempt. The lawyer never told Williams the extent of his private fears. He shared the player's belief that he had become a pawn in a wider game which concerned the making of points about the violence of professional hockey, but he also sensed that the matter had become redolent with other implications, not least political face-saving. Forbes was under no illusions about how badly the attorney general wanted a conviction. At vast public expense McMurtry had failed to convict Detroit's Dan Maloney in a similar case. The Williams case had been thrown out at the preliminary hearing, but McMurtry, ironically a notably fierce performer when he was on the University of Toronto hockey team, had insisted the Crown continue the prosecution. Williams was his last chance for the good headlines.

Forbes knew that if he put his client in the box, the chances were that Williams would lash out at men he regarded as intruders into a way of life that had given him everything he possessed, both materially and in the matter of personal pride. Tiger Williams was on trial because of the way he played the game, the game as he had always known it. And without it, what would he be?

King Clancy came to court with me each day. His wife was dying of cancer, and he spent his time between her side and mine. I felt grateful for what he was doing. He said that hockey was his life, too, and that I had only done what hockey players had been doing for as long as he could remember. If I was guilty, so was King Clancy, the vice-president of the Toronto Maple Leafs. Clancy kept telling me, "The club can never turn its back on you."

The club owner, Harold Ballard, was also reassuring. Every day he spoke to me before I went to the courthouse. He asked whether I needed anything, maybe babysitters for my son, Ben, because Brenda was in the hospital expecting our second child. I heard later that Ballard paid out $80,000 in legal fees. As far as I was concerned, it was an extremely good deal for everybody. I needed a man of Tom Forbes's experience. It was clear to me right away that the whole game was on trial. I was just the poor schmuck caught with the smoking gun.

Nobody had ever said to me, "Go and get number eight!" or "Fix that sonofabitch Joe Blow." Not ever. Not back on the river, not in Peewee or Bantam or Midget, not even in Junior or in professional hockey. It was something you knew, instinctively. You didn't need anyone to draw pictures, to tell you what you had to do to get on in the game. For someone like me it couldn't have been more simple. I fought — or I disappeared.

Red Kelly, my first coach at Toronto, was one of life's gentlemen. He won the Lady Byng Trophy four times. He had been an all-star both at centre and defence. He was an intelligent man and there was a touch of the aristocrat. I used to think sometimes that Red Kelly was cut out for higher things than pro hockey — even though he once served in the House of Commons. But Red never had any trouble telling you it was time to do the business out on the ice. He had this favourite phrase when a game was tight. He would march along the bench saying, "Carriers of water don't chop wood in this game." He would pause for a second and then ask, his voice raised just a bit, "Are the choppers chopping?" You had to be pretty dumb not to react when Red Kelly asked this question. This was a man who never showed a hint of violence away from the rink. He never swore. You knew his mood was bitter if he said, "Hang it!" or, "What the hang's going on?" He was a model guy with a model family. Lanny McDonald called his daughter after Kelly's wife Andra. Kelly was very good to me, settled me down in the big league, gave me plenty of ice time. I think he could see clearly that I understood that in the pros there were no half measures. At that time, ten years ago, you

11

only needed to do one of the important things well. You needed a good shot or great stickhandling, or you had to be able to fight. You had to either carry the water or chop the wood, really well. At the end of my first year Red Kelly knew that he would have no problems with me attending to the woodpile.

For me, hockey fighting was a natural thing. At whatever level, amateur or professional league, I was involved in a fight in my first game. But I suppose it was the business in Los Angeles in 1975 that first made me a marked man with the powers that be. It was a playoff game at the Forum. The Kings had had their best year, got nearly 100 points with people like Bob Berry and Dan Maloney. The fans were pressing against the glass, screaming, super-hyped. In the third period, with things very tense, Rogie Vachon came out of his goal to field the puck, and I just ran over him. Gene Carr skated into me and we dropped the gloves. After the fight, as I was going to the penalty box, there was a terrible commotion. With a general fracas going on, Dave Hutchison, who hadn't played in the game but was the Kings' designated hit man, tried to give me the stick.

We had this sword fight, whittling our sticks down, and then a fan jumped into the box. I had so much adrenalin that I laid into this fan, who was trying to attack me, and it was around about then that the benches cleared and we seemed to be on the verge of a full-scale riot. Some policemen got hold of me and one of them said, "For your sake, I hope we get out of here." They took me to the dressing room and locked the door. I was in there with a huge black cop. Outside, fans were hammering on the door, screaming my name. The cop could see that I was getting a little anxious and he pulled his pistol out of its holster and laid it on his lap. He said to me, "Don't worry, boy, if anybody comes through that door I'll blow his brains out." It was good to hear.

You don't take pride in incidents like that. You do certain things like hitting a goalie and you know the risks, what could result from it. It is a very calculated thing, and you either have the nerve for it or you don't.

In Toronto later, when I went to the courtroom, I was pretty sure that most Canadians would understand the nature of the game and my part in it. As it happened the incident

12

McMurtry's men had got me on was quite innocent, despite all the blood. The cops who had been given the season tickets to look out for bad examples of violence just didn't understand the game, or at least the part of it that most involved someone like me. My lawyer made two big decisions, and he got them both right. He decided to go for trial by judge rather than jury when he found out who the judge would be. Judge Locke was a manly kind of guy, so Tom said that we should go with him. We didn't want to wind up with a couple of broads or some wimp on the jury, who had never seen a game of hockey and who might faint at the sight of blood. Our other crucial victory was that we got a ruling that film could only be offered in evidence if it was run at normal speed. Tom won this point on the grounds that in slow motion, film can suggest deliberation which in reality just didn't exist.

The Owchar incident would have been just another piece of rough hockey if I hadn't been slightly off balance and he hadn't fallen into my stick at the moment of impact. It was a routine situation: Owchar cross-checked me as I went over the blueline, and I went to retaliate by cracking him in the midsection, which is well padded. I didn't aim for his head, which wasn't protected by a helmet. I had been involved in many worse incidents.

Throughout the case I felt a lot of tension. As the legal arguments went back and forth, my vocabulary also improved dramatically. Mostly, we avoided talking to the press and the radio and television guys, but on the odd occasion, one of them would get hold of me and I would make some kind of crack, something like, "I hope it's over soon because I can't go on buying a new suit every day." Some people told me that I had come across as very cool, but it was an act. Some days my shirt was wet with sweat. I kept thinking that some guys had come into my life and were trying to wreck it. I had responsibilities, another hungry mouth on the way. I had a hunger too, for this life that I'd won from hockey, and I wanted it to go on. I had a lot of plans that were now in jeopardy.

I kept telling myself that whatever happened I wouldn't let it break me, not as it had broken Danny Maloney when they got him into court for the incident with my teammate Brian Glennie. I was disgusted by that Glennie business, which was part of the whole deal that had me in court later. Glennie faked

13

unconsciousness. I know, I was there. But it was enough for McMurtry to get Maloney into court. They asked Danny Maloney whether he was cruel to his kids, whether he beat up on his wife. Maloney was a hard-nosed hockey player, but off the ice he was a decent, ordinary guy. Like me, he had grown up in hockey. His coaches had asked him questions about the level of wood chopping.

In court, when they started to ask Maloney about the way he treated his family you could see that something inside him snapped. To play hockey the way Maloney did and the way I have done for ten years now, you have to be very sure of yourself and what you are doing. And if you are not so sure the last thing you ever do is let anyone know about it. You cannot afford to look around or listen to people. There has to be a part of you that is completely shut off. They got inside Maloney in the courtroom in Toronto. They didn't get their conviction but they did get a lot of headlines, a lot of attention. And in the process, they did a lot of damage to a guy who played rough hockey, because that's the way he was told to play if he wanted the paycheques to keep coming.

I thought about Danny Maloney a lot at my own trial. I thought about a lot of things, but I kept coming back to him: how Glennie had been so ashamed of his behaviour on the ice that he wouldn't even go to court, and how all this taxpayers' money was going into the business of prosecuting hockey players. It seemed to me that a lot of people had got their priorities screwed up. There was murder and rape and all kinds of corruption going on outside this courtroom, but here they were, $250,000 into the public purse, trying a case that had already been thrown out at an earlier stage in the investigation. There were times when I felt very close to lashing out, but then I told myself that if they got to Danny Maloney they were not going to get to me.

I had been slightly involved in the Maloney-Glennie affair in that game with Detroit. After Maloney knocked Glennie down, I ran at him — and was sent to the penalty box. But the cops in the stands were looking for some serious injury, something that looked dramatic on film. Glennie's situation looked dramatic but it wasn't.

He had hit Dennis Hextall but when Maloney came in to hit him he fell down and stayed down. There was no doubt that

14

Maloney was very anxious to beat the crap out of Glennie, but whenever he tried to haul him up from the ice, Glennie slipped back down as Maloney kept losing his grip on the sweater. In court they said that Maloney had been banging Glennie's head on the ice, right up to the point of unconsciousness. It wasn't so. I saw everything that happened. There were no marks on Glennie. When he refused to go to court for Maloney's trial, I wasn't surprised.

It's hard to argue against those who say there was too much violence in the game back then. It had reached a peak, and no doubt the peak often seemed too high. But there were other ways of dealing with it apart from looking for a few scapegoats and running up a lot of publicity for certain individuals. There was a hell of a lot of hypocrisy involved. Violence had always been part of the game but now they were isolating a few guys like Maloney and me and heaping all the blame on us. It was so ridiculous when you thought about it. That was the time when all the guys used to sit around and talk about how so-and-so was so damned tough. You never heard about how this guy had a great wrist shot or was a beautiful stickhandler. What you heard about was the size of his fists and how willing he was to use them.

You got pushed into certain attitudes, whether you liked it or not. One of those attitudes was that you never showed a hint of weakness, never thought of apologizing if you should give a cheapshot to the wrong guy, which happened sometimes. You had to keep hard-faced, always. The result was a lot of unhealthy stuff, particularly when the Philadelphia Flyers were built up as the Broad Street Bullies.

As I saw it, there were quite a few mythical hard men on that Philadelphia team. It was kind of pathetic to see how some of those hard men fared when they were cut from the pack at the Spectrum. I'm thinking particularly of people like Orest Kindrachuk and Don Saleski. When Saleski went to Colorado, he took some beatings because in Philadelphia, with the wolf pack around him, he was a big street guy. On his own, it was a different story. We were looking for guys like that when Philadelphia broke up and we got them. I would classify them as guys who like to play tough, do a lot of mouthing off when they have a couple of gorillas at their side.

If there is going to be some violence in a game like hockey, and I think there always will be, it has to be spontaneous, a reaction to circumstances in that game. I get tired of fighting the same people, maybe some numb-brained character who can't play regularly, someone who only dresses for a game when you dress, and whose job is to prove to his teammates that he is tougher than you. It can become wearisome.

There are other kinds of rivalries, those rooted in mutual respect, and I thought of some of those, too, when the lawyers made their points in the courtroom in Toronto. I thought of Terry O'Reilly. If I had gone into the box in the courtroom and told them all about the game, the good and the bad — how it was that men who loved their wives and their children, who were kind to dogs, could leave each other looking like raw meat in the course of a night's work — I would probably have told about the night O'Reilly saved me from serious injury. O'Reilly and I fought every game. We were in the same division and we never missed a chance. One weekend, we played Boston in Maple Leaf Gardens, then went to Boston Garden the following Thursday. In Toronto, Bobby Orr was carrying the puck right along the boards and around our net when I caught him with a great hit, heavy but clean, that must have taken something out of him. On Thursday in Boston, they dropped the puck and almost before it hit the ice O'Reilly and I were at it. We got into a series of fights, and in between these battles with O'Reilly I was running at all the Bruins. The way I saw it, I had nothing to lose. Eventually, O'Reilly had me down on the ice and Wayne Cashman was trying to kick me in the head with his skates. He got one in through my helmet, leaving a deep cut which required six stitches. But it was obvious he wasn't going to leave it at that. It was then that O'Reilly said, low enough to escape Cashman's hearing, "put your head under my body, I'll shield you." I guess he believed that Cashman was capable of kicking my eyes out.

After that incident, I always played O'Reilly even-steven; I would never elbow him, cheap-shot him. It would be hard but clean. O'Reilly had protected me, put his arms over me, but he wouldn't have said, "Hey, Cash, don't do that!" because it would have involved some loss of face. That's how it works within the game. Cashman might have gone into the dressing room and said something like, "Hey, you wimp O'Reilly, what's going on between you and Williams?" Because of the need to protect his standing in the dressing room, O'Reilly did all he could by warning me and shielding me, and he hoped that I wouldn't tell anyone in my own dressing room. A guy with a reputation for toughness wouldn't want people to think he was softening, slipping.

Reputation was everything in those days, and I suppose if I had gone into the box to explain to the Ontario attorney general the inner workings of professional hockey and my own approach, I might have had some difficulties. I wonder how I could have explained the way it was for me going into Philadelphia, when that was supposed to be the toughest place in hockey.

There's no doubt a lot of guys suffered on the way to the ice at the Spectrum. The Broad Street thing got to them before they even laced up their skates. But it never affected me like that. Before the game I was ready to fly, even though I probably hadn't slept much the night before. My bed used to be soaked in sweat. I went out wanting everybody to pick a fight with me: Dave Schultz, Moose Dupont, Bobby Clarke. It didn't matter to me. It seemed to me that every TV camera in the world was in Philadelphia for those games. I was so pumped up I didn't care if I was hit. I was as game as hell in Philadelphia. My reasoning was that if you could do it there, you didn't have to do it so much anywhere else. Boston was different, trickier. They had Cashman and O'Reilly and Kenny Hodge, Bobby Schmautz and Stan Jonathan. Schmautz could fight, but he would sooner spear you. Sometimes you wondered whether he was going to pick your eyes out. Hodge was a big, tough guy who did a lot for a couple of years and then went quiet but you were never sure whether he was going to produce something. You couldn't really relax with him. By comparison, Philadelphia was straightforward.

Schultz was their big man, but I was never overly impressed with him. He struck me as an outright bully. I was never afraid of him, even though he was big for me and forced me to go inside, as a lot of guys did. Once, when he seemed to have the whip hand, I bit him on the end of his nose. I've never seen any films of classic fights involving Schultz. I don't think I ever hurt him with my fists but then he never hurt me. He had a big advantage over me in build, but I had my conditioning. There was never a time when the guys gathered around me in the dressing room and said, "You beat the crap out of Schultz" but then there were occasions when I thought to myself, "You did well, you showed you didn't give anything for his reputation." When you're dealing with a reputation like Schultz's it is important to challenge, make gestures.

When Schultz left the game, he blamed all the violence on his coach, Fred Shero, but we could all say that. What Schultz lacked in the end was mental toughness. He didn't stay the course. It was the same with a lot of those Philadelphia guys.

I could have told the court a few things about the realities of life for a hockey player and no doubt Tom Forbes was right. I would probably have hanged myself if I'd gone into the witness box. I could have told the court about the old arena in Weyburn, how the cold went into your bones and you tried to warm yourself up on the old boiler; and how it was in Junior, up in Flin Flon, or in Estevan — what it was like having grown men shout to you on the ice that when you came off they were going to smash you in the face. You got more fighting than you ever needed in Junior and that was just a training course, a weeding out, for the big league.

The court should really have known about someone like Bob Gassoff. He was probably the meanest hockey player I ever knew. A lot of professionals slept easier after Gassoff died in an accident riding his motorbike down a country lane following a party at Garry Unger's house. I fought Gassoff for about five years. We played together briefly in Junior in Vernon, B.C. In practice we used to spear each other and guys would sit around drinking beer and debating which one of us was toughest. I played against him in Junior, the minor professional league and the NHL, and he never got easier. He would do anything to get an advantage: gouge your eyes, kick, spear, even push his finger into your nose and twist it to increase the pain. He was mentally tough in a way that Dave Schultz will never know about. And there were a lot of things about hockey which the people running that courtroom in Toronto would never know, and maybe wouldn't have been able to understand.

There was much about the courtroom that *I* didn't understand. One lunchtime, at the end of a morning session, I heard

18

my lawyer say to the prosecuter, McGee, "Yeah, I'll see you over there . . ."

I followed Tom Forbes into a bar near the courthouse. Tom sat down with McGee over a drink. I couldn't believe what I was seeing — what kind of scam was this?

"What the hell is going on?" I asked Tom Forbes. He has since told me that he saw the anger and maybe the confusion on my face.

Tom said to me, "It's the same deal as you and Danny Maloney. Three years ago you used to beat each other up. Now you're buddies. Well, I can talk to McGee out of court but he knows that inside the court I'll always be going for his throat." I trusted my lawyer but I couldn't understand the system. "Listen," he said, "this is a very important case for me. Every lawyer in Ontario, maybe Canada, is watching this case. This one is going into the law books. When it's over I want to be in the win column just as badly as you."

Tom Forbes put in a hell of a defence. He showed the court a blown-up picture of Moose Dupont wrapping a stick around my head and said it was a common occurrence, as it was. Our case was simple enough. We said, "Don't give us this bull about a guy getting stitches." A hockey player knew all his life that every time he touched the puck someone was going to try to get it off him by hitting him, maybe knocking him down. Professional hockey players knew that when they went out on to the ice they consented to some form of assault. They knew it from around the age of five or six. Did the attorney general of Ontario want to change the game of hockey, did he want to turn over a new leaf of history just because a guy got hit in the face with a stick and had some stitchwork?

I felt a lot of relief when the judge finally cleared me. There was the relief that I could get on with my career, even though I knew that it would always be hard and that I would be one of those players who had to do a little more to earn their paycheques. I knew that a Bobby Clarke or a Darryl Sittler would always be able to do things which would automatically land me in trouble; that I could only get where I wanted to be if I did the hard, daily work on my physical conditioning and always remembered to chop the wood. I had to be as mentally strong as poor old Bob Gassoff, and maybe I had to adapt a little, too. I had to watch for the Roy McMurtrys — who did not

19

believe in acknowledging their defeats, I noticed. There were no congratulations for us from the other side. They lost as badly as any beat-up hockey team.

The Not Guilty verdict was handed down on October 28. It was also the day King Clancy's wife died and my wife, Brenda, gave me a daughter. Brenda is still bitter about those days but I tell her that they gave me something of an education. We named our daughter Clancy.

2

Roy McMurtry is still the attorney general of Ontario. More remarkable, given McMurtry's political touch and the relentless physical
pressure involved in being a National Hockey League "policeman",
David Williams remains a highly paid player. Unlike Dan Maloney,
Williams left nothing of himself in the Toronto courtroom. It is true that
the game itself has taken some toll, that upon a face which was almost
delicately boyish just a decade ago, a lifetime of conflict has been
impressed. But there is still much robust humour in the face, and the
kind of vitality guaranteed to caution opponents many years younger.

Sit with Williams on the terrace of his West Vancouver house over-
looking the sweep of sea and city and mountains, listen to his vibrant
talk of hunting in Northern British Columbia, of training fierce dogs and
breaking wild horses, and you are reminded of the lines of Ernest
Hemingway. "If people bring so much courage to this world, the world
has to kill them to break them, so of course it kills them. The world
breaks everyone and afterward many are strong at the broken places."
There are those who say that Tiger Williams represents almost everything bad in the game, that he is cynical and self-serving, and that his
talent has been geared exclusively to the business of survival. Certainly he is candid enough about his imperatives. He has a family to
support, a network of dependents tracing back to his prairie roots; and

he will not leave quietly as long as he believes that he can push forward the bridgehead of security he has won from a world which from his first impressions of it never seemed to him overly generous.

Politically, Tiger Williams is some way to the right of Ronald Reagan. Socially, he is amiable and exhaustively involved in charity, and as a responsible member of the community, he has made several spectacular citizen's arrests. Athletically, he admits he is an anarchist. The only obligation on the ice, he says, is this: "Help your guys win."

I don't recognize the term *policeman* as it is applied to those players who have to inject some toughness into their teams. A policeman should be a peacemaker. I've never wanted to be a peacemaker. Big Harold Snepsts is a policeman on the ice. Whenever there is a battle going on, Harold wants it to be "fair." To me, it should never be fair. Someone should have the advantage and he should be using it. The guy who wants it to be fair should look at himself in the mirror and ask himself if he's in the right business.

I've always tried to be quite calculating about the timing of so-called police work on the ice. Obviously, the time to pick a fight is when you're losing. It's remarkable how often it works. A good example of this came at Maple Leaf Gardens one night when the Canadiens were leading us 3–2 with a minute to go. We were pulling our goalie and I happened to be on the ice. I was standing next to Serge Savard and Jimmy Roberts as we waited for a commercial. I started needling them, giving them the stick. The referee didn't see what was happening. When the puck was dropped, I charged into both of them, and we scored almost immediately. Ronnie Ellis knocked it in. He was all on his own because the Montreal guys were trying to shish kabab me. Afterwards, King Clancy came running down to the dressing room. "That's the way I used to do it for the Ottawa Senators in 1932," he said. Of course, sometimes it can backfire.

It backfires mostly when you're physically tired and, because of the fatigue, you've gotten sloppy in your thinking. Maybe you say, "Oh, what the hell, I'm not going to take that from this guy," and he's up for the incident, ready for you to make a move; he's been waiting to give you everything he has. I've seen careers end because of such miscalculations, especially in Junior. I've seen kids going into games full of themselves, sure that this was just another small step towards the big time, and they've come off the ice changed. Something has gone out of them.

I've often told teammates, "Don't be dumb, don't stand there and take a beating just because you're scared that people are going to think you're chicken." I've said this to guys who can play the game well, really well, because they are vulnerable to one bad beating. It is the point that Red Kelly made. Different players are built for different jobs. When a guy stands there and gets a bad beating, it creates two problems. One, he is personally demoralised, perhaps destroyed for good. And two, it is terrible for his team. Sometimes you can see the life drain out of a team when one of its men has been hammered. You can see it happen physically.

I took my first bad beating in Bantam. I was playing for the Weyburn Comets down in Francis, a farming hamlet about thirty miles from town. When we played the farmers, we had to make a lot of concessions on the matter of age limitations, because the farmers just didn't have enough players, in this case enough fourteen-year-olds. I'll never forget that night in Francis. It was one of those games that have tremendous pressure. The farmers were very strong and aggressive, and they were much more mature. It was a time when I thought I could beat anybody, and looking back now, I realize that quite a few of my teammates wanted to see me licked.

The farmers had a big guy, a sixteen-year-old, named Brian Merk. He was giving us quite a few problems in front of our net so I speared him. A little later in the game Merk skated alongside me and said, "Don't spear me again or I'll hurt you." Between periods I said to my teammates that I would go right on spearing the hayseed, just as long as he kept coming in front of our net. I did spear him at the first opportunity and he dropped his gloves and started pounding me. While I was in the penalty box Merk's father came over to apologize. Both my eyes were closed. I groped my way out of the box, but they had to lead me to the dressing room. I couldn't play any more that night. I was blind. The following morning my older brother Leonard was shocked when he saw my face. I told him I had made a big mistake. I'd put my head down and the other guy was too strong. I just couldn't get my head up. He had a free target. "Why didn't you turn turtle? Leonard asked me. I said, "No way. I would never do that." I also said that I'd get Merk. I

23

intended to even things up. But he was one of the few guys in non-professional hockey that I never settled the score with.

Sometimes you look at your career and it seems that your whole time is spent settling scores, proving to this guy that you're not scared of him, keeping somebody else under your thumb, always adjusting the balance of power. In a way, this is the reality of it all, even in the era of Wayne Gretzky. We hear a lot about Gretzky being what the modern game is all about and there is no doubt that he is incredible, but then people sometimes forget about Dave Semenko. Amazingly, even Wayne Gretzky sometimes forgets about Semenko. He would never do it while he is playing the game — because everybody knows that Semenko is worth at least 25 goals a season to Gretzky — but when he talks about it rather than does it, well, he can be forgetful.

Gretzky said recently that the age of the tough hockey player was over, that if anybody could explain to him how a bar bell helped you to score goals he would start using one. This was obviously hypocrisy. Gretzky has so much natural talent that he can sail beyond the pressures less gifted players must bear, and his club pay Semenko a tremendous salary simply to look after him. In the 1984 playoffs Semenko proved that he can play hockey, score goals, but that will never be his major role with the Edmonton Oilers. To play Semenko's role, you have to be a rare breed of hockey player, and there is no doubt that he is an unusual character. The club doesn't disguise his job. He gets only sufficient ice time to fulfill his main function, which is to intimidate, and the fans are very free with their abuse. But he seems happy in his work. He's big and mean, and he gives you the impression that he wants to hurt you. I know that he wants to get me, that he really hates me. This is probably because I take every chance I get to run at Gretzky.

If I was to compare myself with a Semenko or a Schultz I would say that I have thought about the game a little more, tried to understand a little more deeply what goes into shaping winners and losers. As I see it, Semenko doesn't have to worry about such matters as timing and psychology. The level of his team's play would make that unnecessary. What he has to do is prepare himself for about five minutes of action per game. He has to gear himself up to go beat the crap out of anyone trying to bother Wayne. What you have to give Semenko is the fact that he is genuinely intimidating. Just by dressing for the game, he provides protection for a player like Gretzky. Semenko is a limited player, but as far as I'm concerned, he is the most valuable Edmonton Oiler after Gretzky — and I'm not forgetting great talents like Mark Messier, Glenn Anderson and Paul Coffey. Without Semenko, there would be a competitive vacuum on the Oiler team.

I have always made it my business to try to fill such vacuums. I've given a lot of thought to the challenge of gaining an advantage. This is probably why I've always gotten on so well with Roger Neilson.

During our Toronto phase, Roger and I had a method for gaining an edge that finally pushed the league into changing a rule. Our tactic was to provoke an opposition player into some kind of retaliation by systematic needling from me when we were on a power play. My objective was to take a guy with me to the penalty box, turn a six–five manpower advantage into a five–four edge. Statistics tell you that there is a dramatic increase in scoring when three players are off the ice. We became notorious for this move. Against Vancouver, it seemed we could always score a goal after I had manipulated someone, usually Harold Snepsts, into the box. I remember that the Vancouver captain, Chris Oddleifson, used to scream at the referee, "Watch Williams, watch Williams."

The only problem for me was that I had to take some shots from the guy I had provoked. I couldn't start the action, couldn't draw a penalty without taking him with me. I had to needle the guy to the point where he reacted, and then defend myself after the fact. I did it because I could see the point of it. It gave us an edge. Then the NHL rules committee said that in this situation the penalties would be served by the offenders but the manpower on the ice would not be affected. The league closed down our racket. We had to go away and think about new ways of finding an edge.

This, I believe, is what the business of professional sport is about. What it means is that you have to be prepared to do whatever is required to make a career, to get the big contract which is going to set you up for the rest of your life. A lot of guys do this but then a lot of them make one mistake. They never toughen themselves for the days when the criticism starts to flow. It is ridiculous but true that some guys never get over the first time they read about themselves being goons. A guy goes home and his wife is crying about the fact that the kids are going to have a tough time in school because of this article in the newspaper. And this can blow a guy's mind. Meanwhile, he's just got a $10,000 cheque for two weeks' work.

I always come back to the money, because you have to be honest. I'm not playing a sport. I'm not playing for fun. I do get fun out of the game — I'm always the first at the rink and the last to leave — but if the general manager of the club called me up today and said that I wouldn't be paid for the next ten games, well, there's no way I would play one shift. I'd tell him that I had hungry mouths to feed. You go along doing things for a purpose. You can't analyze it all too much. I put Stan Mikita out of the game, and maybe Garry Unger but I can't afford to dwell on that. I have to say it could have been the other way around. Mikita was very chippy. I recall thinking, "Well, he didn't give me much option." That was after I'd speared him. Maybe you hide behind a few old truths. Maybe you just say, "We live by the sword, we might just die by it." It is one of the more obvious risks you run when you tell yourself you're going to make a living out of hockey.

You justify yourself in various ways. Only the players I have gone against can confirm or deny what I say here, but I like to think that I have been rough on very few guys who have not deserved some kind of retribution, and that if I have over-stepped the mark against players who had no reputation for violence, it was because of a set of circumstances in a game. I tell myself I did it for the club, because something had to be done, something totally unforeseen by the opposition. Something had to be done to justify my paycheque.

I did it at Quebec City in one of the last games of the 1980–81 season, at the end of my second year in Vancouver. We were scuffling for a playoff spot, which we got only on the last game when Washington lost and we won in Los Angeles. We were leading the Nordiques, who had pulled their goalie in the last minute. Buddy Cloutier came onto the ice and he had been flying that night. He came towards our goal very menacingly; he was my man, and it was a situation in which I felt I had to do something for the team. We needed that win very badly. I speared him, quite viciously. I guess it was a little bit

26

like being in the army. You're not sure he's the Viet Cong but you shoot him anyway. Let's remove the doubt. It isn't pretty, it isn't nice, but I believe it's my function.

Bob Nystrom is a good player but it isn't his stickhandling or his shooting that has kept him with the Islanders for ten years. It's the fact that he gives his teammates confidence. That's the reality. Nystrom will make hard, maybe dirty, decisions — and the Islanders are aware of this. This awareness is a big factor in everything they do.

Coaches may not spell out their requirements. Demands may not be written into your contract. But within the game there is no attempt to blur the reality. When a physical situation has gotten beyond your control — maybe it came at a time when you were physically drained at the end of a shift — your teammates let you know. They make clear their displeasure, their belief that you have let them down. And if you have won a fight, if you have seized some advantage, created some momentum, they also show their pleasure. After the game, they will take you out and order you the biggest steak on the menu and pick up the tab. Darryl Sittler and Lanny McDonald would do this in Toronto, where we had the three-second rule. Sittler and McDonald were supposed to wait three seconds before they reacted to any incident. If I wasn't there in that time they were on their own because it was obvious I had my own troubles. Sittler and McDonald could look after themselves, but why risk your highest scorers? If McDonald broke his hand in a fight our power play was shot to pieces. The fighting was my job.

At first it is very difficult in the NHL simply because you have to make so many decisions and you never get much time. No one is interested in what you did in the last game. It is a case of "What are you going to do for me today, kid?" I accepted that principle. Your confidence can be hit when you take a bad penalty or misjudge a situation, and then people jump all over you. So you have to remind yourself of when you took a run at a guy and he just coughed up the puck and allowed McDonald to score. You have to play little mental games with yourself all the time.

I decided at the beginning of my career that I would follow a certain policy very strictly. I would always go out and give it all

27

I had in games and practices both, whatever the conditions, whether I had a cold or a sore leg or some personal problem, and no one would ever hear me complaining. I figured that this would make all my teammates like me, and that all the people in the stands would feel they were getting their money's worth. And if I was unfortunate enough to get somebody like Punch Imlach managing the team, another club would leap at me. Because there wouldn't be any doubt about what I could do, what I represented. What I represented was an understanding of what it is to be a professional. That's what I told myself when I did the things that some of the other guys would never do.

One of the things you learn most quickly is that hockey is like the rest of the world: it operates on double standards. You see a Bobby Clarke doing something totally vicious and then later someone will say, "Is that Clarke ever determined!" Denis Potvin once speared Jack Valiquette in the face, cut him up very badly, and got two minutes in the box. "Oh, that was Potvin, he didn't mean it, " people said. If you're a big boy you get turned the blind eye because the league president John Ziegler, or the vice-president Brian O'Neill, doesn't want to get involved in public debates with Potvin or Clarke. That wouldn't look too good in the papers. So the safe alternative is to go for someone like me from time to time. As I see it, the goal scorers, the glamour guys, are like the politicians. They sail over the inconveniences of life. If anyone is going to be isolated and attacked, it's not going to be a Potvin or a Clarke. It's going to be some grinder, some poor plugger who's been written off as a goon long ago.

So you have to learn to be very controlled on the ice. You have to know who you are and what you are doing. You can't afford to have any false ideas about yourself. Because of the need for conflict and for a strong front on the ice, you develop two personalities: you have the emotional equipment you need for the game, and then you have to strip that away as you go about your own life. I suppose it is inevitable that sometimes there is some overlapping.

The only time I get ruffled off the ice is when someone directly challenges me, maybe gives me the finger or choke sign. A guy gave me the finger sign one summer's night in Toronto and it led to his imprisonment. I was driving home from Chatham, Ontario. It was very slow on the expressway because of the crowds going to a Blue Jays game. In the next lane, a guy finished a hamburger and threw the wrappings out of his car. I leaned out the window and asked him how he'd like it if I went round to his house and threw garbage in his yard. He didn't say anything, just sat there, hunched over the wheel of his sports car. Then, when the traffic cleared, he gunned his car and gave me the sign. I chased him for about twenty-five miles. He went through stop lights, over curbs. Eventually he pulled into a police station and ran up to the desk shouting, "There's a guy out there who wants to kill me." I went into the station and said that I wanted to make a citizen's arrest. It turned out that the litterbug had a long list of driving convictions and unpaid fines, and he'd been driving while his licence was suspended. The judge sent him down for eighteen months, without parole. He also called me an upright citizen.

Upright citizen? It's true that there are lots of things about life which make me angry. I see a lot of dishonesty, a lot of eagerness to pick up an easy buck. I hate hypocrisy and I can't understand the mentality of people who would toss their garbage into the street. That offends me. I guess some might say that the things I do on the ice are offensive. Well, I've never disguised myself or my intentions. I give my employers value for money, I give Caesar what is his.

When I got my first contract as a twenty-year-old it suddenly occurred to me that I was in a position to earn a million dollars. If I did my work, if I protected my body, if I didn't let a lot of irrelevance creep into my thinking, I could make a good life for myself and for my family. I could help people I wanted to help, I could have the freedom to make choices. And the price? The price was going out on the ice and battling a guy every once in a while. And every so often someone would get the better of me, bend my body a little. So what? So what, when you measure it against the good life and the freedoms I can win in the battle.

It would have been nice winning those freedoms in the fashion of Lanny McDonald, getting the glory of a goal scorer along with them. But that wasn't at my disposal. I guess I was born to do it the hard way.

3

He was born 3 February 1954 in a two-bedroom house on Aylmer Street, the poorest section of Weyburn. The house, down by the grain elevators on the Souris River, is condemned now. He was the third son and fourth child of Elizabeth and Robert Idris "Taffy" Williams. Taffy Williams had come from Wales to make his fortune but in the meantime he worked as a painter at the mental hospital and, when his shift was over, wherever he could find extra work. But however hard he worked he couldn't get ahead. Children accumulated, and each arrival meant another turn of the financial screw within the little house heated by the old oil stove. There were Hugh and Leonard, Ann and David, Morgan and Sid, Heather and Trevor.

After Morgan's arrival, the family moved to a larger house. Their new home was a duplex on Bison Avenue, next door to the Brennans. George Brennan was also an immigrant with a large family; he had seven children. He worked as an orderly at the mental hospital.

"At night," David recalls, "we could hear the Brennans talking in the bedrooms, and they could hear us. But they were good people. They were like us. They were caught in the numbers game. They were stretched to the limits."

Elizabeth Williams went to meetings of the Royal Canadian Legion Ladies Auxiliary on Monday and the Anglican church women's group on Thursday; on Sunday she marched her brood to church, often at temperatures of well below zero Fahrenheit. Otherwise, Elizabeth Williams worked, cleaning the house, waxing the linoleum, patching clothes, canning vegetables. And when Taffy Williams wasn't working, he was giving to his children the one thing he had without limit — enthusiasm. He gave them optimism and a sense that if you were weak you had no chance at all. He taught his kids to fight. It was something important to learn on the prairies, though many of Weyburn's ten thousand townsfolk believed that in the Williams household the lesson had been absorbed a little too intensely, that aggression had been developed to a fault.

Johnny Norman, the town clerk of Weyburn who was David Williams's Peewee hockey coach, says, "Tiger was a Williams all right. Once he refused to play in goal, and I hit him across his legs with a hockey stick; but he didn't sulk, he got on with the game. He was a great fighter by nature. Frankly, I'm surprised he has had the success he has, considering the level of his talent. What you always knew was that once a game started, Tiger wanted to win more than anyone else. I guess he got it from Taffy. I guess it was in the blood."

A lot of things got to me as a kid. I used to hate it when my mother had to patch our pants into the small hours of the morning or do the ironing after bringing the laundry in from outside, where it was thirty below and made the clothes like pieces of plywood. We didn't have a goddamned drier.

We didn't have a car, either, for a long time. Then we got one, for a short time. My brother Hugh, who was a lot older than the rest of us, rolled it, and it was a write-off. It burned me to see that happen to the new car my dad had battled so long to get. Losing the car really put us behind the eight ball. For one thing, it meant that we had to walk to church on Sunday mornings, and when it was really cold, that was one of the last things you wanted to do. But we all knew how important our church-going was to Mum. It pleased her so much if she could get us all there. It set her up for the week. Today, I sometimes think I should be doing the same thing with my kids, but a hockey player's schedule is difficult; it's hard to have a routine. I'm not sure she would understand this.

Another thing we didn't have was a TV. We used to walk through the snowdrifts to watch "Gunsmoke" at the McCarthy place down the block. Mr. McCarthy would give us certain

31

nights when we could go around. "Gunsmoke" was my favourite — I fell in love with Miss Kitty — but I would have watched anything. After the show was over, we all hoped old man McCarthy would let us stay. But he would usually say, "Okay, Williams clan, it's time to go," and we would have to troop out and trample a snowbank to death on the way home. I used to think, "Wait till I get my goddamned colour set."

There were so many things that nagged at me. Not having a car for so many years, nor a telephone, put you at the mercy of other kids when it came to hockey. If I didn't get a lift or the use of a telephone I was finished. To get a message about changes in practice times or about special games, such as an all-star or Representative game, I had to leave the telephone number of the grocery store or a neighbour's house and then check with them at a certain time. It took a lot of planning, and you could wear yourself out collecting messages.

And there were the skates and the sticks. My dad bought me a pair of skates that he thought were the greatest skates in the world and I said how good they were. But what I wanted was CCM Tackebury skates. "Tacks" were big time. They were what the guys in the NHL used. My dad always did what he could for us but I never did get the Tacks, until I was able to go out and buy my own. It seemed to me that all the other guys had the good sticks. Sometimes I would get hold of a broken stick at the rink and take it home for repair; sometimes I'd just take one that hadn't been glued to the floor. Some might say that was stealing. I said it was being in the right place at the right time. It was quite a job with the broken sticks. My dad used to get me special nails from the hospital workshop but it was hard driving them into the fibreglass. You put on the glue and then in the morning threw on some tape. Then you went down to the rink and hoped your stick didn't fall apart in your hands. Recently I saw a kid in the Pacific Coliseum in Vancouver pick up the stick of an NHL player. By the way he handled it, you wouldn't have thought it was anything at all. Back in Weyburn, you fought for the broken stick of some Junior player.

When I first started playing organized hockey, in Peewee, I had to play in goal. But I refused to wear a mask. They used to say, "Hey, kid, you've got to wear a mask," and I'd say that I didn't want any wimpy wire mask — Johnny Bower didn't wear a mask. But I wasn't really any good in goal, and so I used to whack a few guys around the net and wander up the ice. It was then that Johnny Norman picked up on the nickname *Tiger*. The next year, I was playing forward, and our team — the Maple Leafs — were given hockey jackets. Printed on the sleeve of my jacket was "Tiger". Everywhere I went I wore that jacket. I'd put half a dozen old sweaters on and then pull on the jacket. I was happy with my nickname. I liked to think it was an exact reflection of my work on the ice. I suppose it became my working name.

My nickname came from the way I played hockey, but what I was most tigerish about, deep down, was the need to earn some money. It hurt that my dad didn't have a car. It hurt like hell, and it was a wound that never really healed. Recently I played in Winnipeg and my dad came to see me after the game. He'd driven five hundred miles to watch me play — and to show me his new car.

When I was starting out in hockey, one of the things that kept me going was the idea of that new car in the future. A lot of that early hockey was filled with stops and starts, and that was hard for someone like me, a labourer on skates. But it couldn't kill me off. I'd skate beside some local hotshot kid, and he wouldn't get the better of me, because I had this driving force. I'd say to myself, "My old man's going to have a better car than this guy's old man, because I'm going to buy the son of a bitch."

It amazes me today looking at the television commercials for the airlines: *Feeling jaded? Take a trip to Hawaii or Florida.* When I was growing up you never dreamed about holidays like that. They were something you saw on other people's television sets.

What I used to look forward to was going to my Uncle Fred's farm a hundred miles down the road at Storthoaks on the U.S.-Manitoba border. That was a hell of a trip. I would throw bales of hay into the wagons, clear away rocks from the fields. Guys would say, "What the hell are you doing that for without pay?" I couldn't really understand the question. There were quite a few reasons. It was good for my mother's family and for ours. It saved them labour costs and we would get meat for the winter. It was good for my strength. It would be good for my hockey — I realized that right away. When I was fourteen years old, it was nothing for me to spend the day throwing around bales that weighed between forty and sixty-five

33

pounds. We would move about forty thousand bales in a two-week period. Also, I thought farmers were big-time guys. They got to use all that great, powerful machinery. For quite a long time, it was a dream of mine to go back to the prairies and buy a farm. When I was with Toronto, my Uncle Fred would come down to Los Angeles for our games there, and I would say to him, "I'm coming back to buy you guys out, and you're going to work for me."

Of course, the dream died when I looked at the modern-day realities. You have to pay $100,000 for a tractor and another $100,000 for a combine harvester that you only use for three weeks. If you have broken-down machinery, you can't make the profit, because the frost settles in so quickly. It was a good dream, though, and I often think of those days in the fields. It was wonderful to feel yourself growing stronger every day, and at the end of it you had the potatoes and the beef and the chickens for the winter.

The most significant thing about the summer was that there was no hockey. It was as though normal life was suspended. You could goof around the pool hall, let off a little steam. Dad would give you a cuff or two for getting into trouble, but the only time he got really mad was if the police were involved. I think he realized we had a reputation to keep up.

Yes, we were proud of our reputation. I guess my dad set the pattern. When he arrived in Canada, he had this strong Welsh accent, so he had to stand up for himself, and Hugh followed very strongly in his footsteps. As far as we were concerned, there was no one tougher than us; and if there was, well, we said just find 'em and we'll straighten it all out. Everybody was scared of Hugh. Even the cops. They wouldn't come to the house to talk to him unless my dad was there. My dad was a pal of the police chief, Todd Williams, who was also from Wales. I guess we put a little bit of a strain on that friendship. Hugh once bit a policeman's ear half off. The policeman wore a scarf over the wound for quite a while. Then he got a plastic ear.

Hugh had left home when I was just growing up, getting to find out about certain basic things in life; but he left his legacy. He was a tough character, all right, and for a long time I modelled myself on him. He was the kind of guy who could walk into a room and say, "Jump!" and everyone would say,

34

"How high?" He wasn't a model brother, but when I was a kid, I thought he was the greatest thing I'd ever seen. He would come back to Weyburn in a Cadillac or a Mercedes and he always got good pay in the construction business.

I suppose the thing that drew me most strongly to Hugh was that he wanted so much from life. When I was a kid, Hugh was the hero. He was so strong, so fearless, and he always had great looking broads. He did nothing as a hockey player, scarcely laced up a pair of skates, but I forgave him that because I felt he could do anything he wanted. Things that weighed down other guys just bounced off him.

Hugh gave me my first set of weights. He fashioned them out of pipes left by workmen who had been installing natural gas at our house. He took the pipes, scrounged some weights from a grain elevator, and late at night stole some coke boxes from a local grocery store. The coke boxes formed the bench. It was a more than adequate set of weights. That was typical of him. I imagined that he could get in a spaceship and figure out the way to fly it. He might hit a few curbs before taking off, but I would have backed him to succeed.

Eventually he came out of the fast lane. His first marriage failed. But Hughie could always make something out of nothing. He rebuilt his life; he found a fine woman and married again. Some guys in Saskatoon bought the local pool hall and asked him to fix it up, put in video machines and stuff like that. And he did such a good job he got a partnership and eventually he got enough money to invest in a hotel in Whitehorse in the Yukon. The idea was to make a million out of the pipeline workers. But the pipeline never came off, and Hugh's partners pulled out. He seems to be happy enough running the hotel. Only Hugh could sell a room to a rich old American couple and say how nice and quiet the place was, while he had blood on his face after throwing a bunch of drunks out of the beer parlour downstairs. But then, I always say to him that you need to have been hit in the head by a slapshot to live in Whitehorse.

It was always clear that Leonard was going to be the scholar of the family, the guy who would give my mother her proudest moments. When she was sick, we took her from the hospital for Leonard's graduation. We had to carry her into the hall for the ceremony, but it was worth it for her because Leonard had carried off every prize or scholarship available to him in the

35

twelfth grade. Mum's face glowed with pride that night. She always wanted at least one or two of us to succeed in school and Leonard came up big. He went off to the University of Saskatchewan, got two degrees and came back to teach in the Weyburn high school. He teaches history and geography, which, along with beating the crap out of people, were always family strongpoints. In some areas Leonard's temperament differs from mine, but I will always respect him for his knowledge and hard work, plus the fact that he put our mother in such good spirits, and he is a fierce competitor.

Once we organized a family reunion and we had a series of tournaments, including tennis. Leonard brought a trophy for the tennis and it was inscribed: "Len Williams–champion." I couldn't believe it when I saw that, but I suppose I shouldn't have been too surprised. Another time, one hot summer's night, we played tennis in Weyburn and he beat me badly. The following day he was mouthing off about his victory, and it really got to me. The next night we played again, and we agreed the winner would get a hundred bucks. Leonard had suggested the bet when he was leading 3–0. He was a better player than me, but I was so determined to get the better of him after all that mouthing and cockiness that eventually I won the set. He didn't show any signs of giving me the hundred bucks, so when he went to shower, I slipped his watch into my pocket. Later that night, he called me up to ask if I'd seen his watch. I said, yes, it was on my wrist, and it would stay there until I got my hundred bucks. I'm still wearing the watch.

Leonard was a provincial boxing champion and a very hard linebacker in high school football; and once he got some teeth knocked out playing goal in hockey. He wasn't much of a goalie, but he understood the game very well. When I played Junior, he was always on the phone telling me about ways I could improve my game. In some ways he reminds me of Roger Neilson: he has the kind of brain that takes in theories very easily. But sometimes I don't appreciate his advice, even though I know that deep down he is a fan of mine. I've explained to him that now I have two coaches, two professionals, and that when I come out of a dressing room, I don't want to hear about the pass I missed at the 7:03 mark of the second period. I think now he understands how these things can get to you after a game.

36

When Morgan was a kid, I decided he was a wimp. He would sit around all day reading a set of war books my dad had got by mail order. Sometimes we needed a guy for the hockey games we played on the backyard rink, but he was always reading. It used to drive me crazy and more than once I would give him a swat or two, but it didn't make any difference to him. He would just go back to his books. Anything about war, Morgan could tell you. You'd be having supper and he would start talking about some jerk of an Englishman who did something in the Boer War. He was such a gentleman.

Even when he became a national boxing champion, he always seemed short of true Williams aggression. He might be fighting some tough looking guy, and I would say, "Why the hell don't you try to intimidate these guys? Tell them you're going to break them into little pieces." He would just shake his head. He told me he wanted to win with intelligence and style. He said you could get there being a nice guy — with hard work. And the truth was that he was a nice guy and a real hard worker. He would go down to the cold, small gym and work out all on his own, his breath steaming and sweat on his brow. Morgan was different, but he proved many times over that he wasn't a wimp. Now he works with juvenile delinquents. He has a very good family life.

Trevor, who came after Morgan, was the Williams boy hit hardest by our mother's death. Really, it devastated his life. It was hard for all of us: Ann, the eldest girl; and young Heather and baby Sid; but Trevor just retreated into himself. For a while, you had to wonder whether he would come out of it. He went off to Saskatoon, where he went to high school. Eventually, he got himself together and became a provincial boxing champion. He picked up the pieces, but for some time his life was empty.

We all felt a bit of that emptiness. When Mum went, she left a hell of a hole in all our lives. Today, when they play the national anthem before a game, I always think of her and I ask her to look after me.

My mother took sick one night at the rink, where she had come to watch me play hockey. She was just outside the dressing room, bent double, and her stomach was as though she was pregnant. She was in such terrible pain that the doctor thought she had a perforated ulcer. They rushed her to the hospital and opened her up; they found out then that she had cancer. She was moved to a cancer ward in Regina about a hundred miles from home, and most nights I would go to the hospital with my dad. That's how I learned to drive. Dad would be so tired from work and all the travelling, he would be fighting to stay awake as we drove home from the hospital. It would usually be around midnight. I was only fourteen years old, but I had driven tractors down on the farm. I kept saying, "Why don't you let me take over? Have a sleep in the back." One night, he was so damned tired he pulled off the road and said, "You'd better take over."

The house was so empty with my mother gone. Ann went away to train as a psychiatric nurse in Selkirk, Manitoba. Trevor, Sid and Heather would have to come home from school at lunchtime and make themselves jam sandwiches. We did what we could, but the little ones were left on their own a lot. It was hard, because my mother had done everything. When she was there, you could come into our house at 10:00 A.M. any day and the floors would be gleaming and every bed would be made. I always said she made the best meals and provided the cleanest clothes a kid ever had.

Two incidents that came in the first days after my mother's death stick in my mind. Before the funeral, Ann was attempting to beautify the house, clear away the rubbish which had accumulated with Mum away in the hospital. In the process she had thrown away the treasures of my life. She had tossed out the model planes and cars I had collected with my dad, and also all the hockey and baseball cards I had so patiently begged and traded for. I was so bitter. The real pain was in my mother's death, but it was as though it was coming out through the business of the models and the cards.

The hockey cards were most important to me. I had been proud of my ability to trade for great players. Because it was usually the Montreal and Toronto games shown on television, it was possible to trade one Canadien or Maple Leaf for three or four guys from New York or Chicago. That's how I built up my collection. I would read all the bull about the New York and Chicago guys in the magazines and sports pages. I also had a few friends in school who didn't have so many kids in the family, and they often had the odd quarter in their pockets, and sometimes they would buy me a packet of gum. I would throw the gum away. I didn't want gum — I wanted the pictures of great hockey players. I would be on one of those cards one day.

When Ann threw away the cards and the models, it was as though she had thrown away part of my life; and with Mum gone, it seemed like everything was falling apart. School didn't make it any better. At the end of one afternoon session with a student teacher, he told me to clear away my desk. I put away my books, and then he said I had to do the whole row. I told him he must be joking. He seemed like the kind of guy who is very conscious of his position of authority, and he had been some kind of football star at the University of Saskatchewan. I told him not to ride me, but he kept on insisting I clear away the whole row of desks. I guess something just welled up in me. I let him have it. I gave him some very heavy shots, and then I picked up my jacket and left the school. Years earlier, I had thrown a bottle of cleaning liquid at a teacher, and my dad had been forced to go down to talk to the principal. On this last occasion the whole incident was put down to my mother's death. Nothing was said to me, because there was really no point. School had never been a big area for me. If I was going to get anywhere in the world, it wasn't going to be through a schoolbook.

At school, I guess I failed my mother. But when she died, I made a vow. I told her I would look after the troops.

4

It was a vow more easily made than accomplished by a fifteen-year-old who had scorned even the foothills of an orthodox education. To most people in Weyburn Tiger Williams was shaping up not as a winner, a provider for a family suddenly without anchor, but a loser, angry at the hardships and injustices of life. His violence seemed to go beyond the needs of hockey. It seemed to be an expression of deep hurts.

Even hockey, the arena in which his hopes were highest, seemed unpromising. His Bantam hockey coach, Jerry Murray, had to fight off committeemen and parents who demanded that he be removed from the team. The claim was that Williams was involved in too much riotous behaviour both on and off the ice. He was simply too extreme.

Williams declared that one day he would make it to the NHL. He would come back to Weyburn a rich man. His father would have a fine car, and so would he. He would have a colour television set in every room. He would take holidays in Florida and Hawaii. It was all there; it was just waiting for him to stake his claim. He told this to anyone who would listen. Mostly the listeners laughed.

Jerry Murray could be quite a crude character. He wasn't of the Red Kelly school. He bellowed and screamed and sometimes his language was very rough. But I never wanted to let him

40

down. He stood there outdoors in temperatures as low as thirty below and coached you. He showed some faith. A lot of people wanted me off the team because of the shenanigans I created, the millions of penalties I took. But Murray always stood by me. He said that he knew he could count on me when the going was rough. He was the first guy, apart from my dad and my brothers, who went to bat for me. If it wasn't for Jerry Murray, I could have been tossed to one side. So I owed him a debt. I paid it with interest.

We travelled in an old red and white school bus all over Saskatchewan. Once the bus broke down on some deserted highway and we nearly froze to death. We waited for hours before a farmer came by and helped us fix the hose. On another occasion some antifreeze was spilled over the uniform bag, and for a whole season, we played with antifreeze stains on our shirts. We looked like a bunch of aliens, but it didn't affect our play.

We made the playoffs, and in a tournament in West Kildonan in Winnipeg, we won the Cougar and took it back to the team's little glass trophy case in Weyburn. The tournament was played in an outdoor arena. I had never been so cold playing hockey. We took our extra socks, cut eye-holes in them and pulled them over our heads. We changed goalies about every two minutes, because that was as long as anyone could stand in the net. The wind was blowing so hard that there were huge snowdrifts in the corners of the rink. But none of that mattered when we won.

Often my dad would drive the bus. The other guys hated it when he showed up for a trip, because they knew that if we lost, he would refuse to put the heater on for the drive home. Before a road game, the guys would ask him if he was coming; if he said he wasn't sure, someone would say under his breath, "Hell, I hope not, he'll freeze our bugs off." I used to say there was an easy solution to the problem. All we had to do was win the goddamned game. Sometimes Dad would growl, "If I'm going to drive this bus all the way to some little hick town, you bastards better win." We didn't lose too many games, but when we did, we knew what to expect. I've never met a worse loser than my dad.

But he was always good to be with, and when I was just a little kid, in the summer I used to hike out to the hospital

41

where he worked. I tried to get there at lunchtime, when he would buy me a Fanta. One of his moonlighting jobs was equipment manager at the hockey arena, and he worked as an usher at the Junior games. One night he promised a couple of friends that he would squeeze them into the kids' area at the end of the rink, where it was about two thousand degrees below; but another usher, Doug McKenzie, tried to throw them out. My dad dropped him.

The next day, I was in Jimmy Rose's barbershop, and while he was cutting my hair, he said, "Your old man shouldn't have hit Doug McKenzie. Doug would have hit him back if he hadn't known your dad has a bit of trouble with his heart."

I was just fuming. I said, "Well, one thing my old man taught me was that you always get in the first punch, and that's what happened last night."

If I'd ever played in a way that might have caused my old man to believe we had lost because of my lack of effort, well, I just wouldn't have gone home. He would have beaten me. I wouldn't have been able to sit down for a month. Even now, I think of my old man when my team have lost a game and played poorly. I think of him when I see a couple of teammates talking to opposition players who have just walked over us. I get a flash of anger. I think of what Dad would say.

Dad had always been my conscience when I was a kid, right back to the days on the river. I would feel his eyes on me. I would want to stand out, show him that no one was going to push Taffy Williams's kid around. My old man had been in the army. He was a scrapper. He was my inspiration.

And there were provocations, too. There was the provocation of kids with better sticks and better skates, kids who laughed at me when I said that I was going to make it to the Western Hockey League and then on the NHL. They had little luxuries in their lives, luxuries like potato chips and Coca Cola, while I was stuck with meat and potatoes. But I told them it was going to be different. I told this to kids like Billy Shupe. His family owned an implements business and his uncle Jack coached in Junior hockey. He was a decent kid but he had a lot of things I wanted.

I would tell somebody like Billy Shupe that I was going to have a Cadillac and a house right next to the hockey rink. I'd never have to walk to the rink, never have to go into the teeth of the east wind. I was very conscious of that wind, with all the walking I did to the rink, and to church on Sundays. In Weyburn, the winter wind only blew in one direction. If it blew from the east, it brought snow and rain, and if it didn't blow at all, you knew there was going to be a storm with hailstones as big as coffee cups. First, I was going to get my Cadillac to drive to the rink, then I would get my big house by the rink. When I got my house, I would use the Cadillac to drive to the pool hall. Back then, hockey was my life — and the pool hall was my diversion.

You knew the pool hall was filled with dead-enders and punks, but they were the guys all the stories were about. They were the characters, the real characters. The other guys, who went to the school dances in suits and with slick hair, were the weirdos. There was something wrong with those guys, something missing. They were the kids who wore scarfs in the winter.

Weyburn was a typical prairie town: a main street, a couple of stop lights, a baseball diamond, the hockey rink and the pool hall. They had a rule that you couldn't go in the pool hall until you were sixteen years old, but I used to hang around and wheedle my way in.

There was always a bit of drama at the pool hall. They used to play a little poker and farmers would come in with their grain cheques; quite a bit of money was lost down there. Quite a bit of blood was spilled, too. Sometimes someone would say to me, "Hey Tiger, some guy's just beaten the crap out of my brother," and we'd go gown to the pool hall looking for trouble. When old Henry Yeik ran the place, he banned our clan because he thought we had been into the till, but we had never taken a damned thing.

Sometimes you would get into a pool game for quite high stakes. You'd double up to about five or six bucks, and then if you won, it would be quite a job getting the money; so you often had to beat the guy with a cue. Once, I cracked a guy over the head with a cue, and old Henry chased me right out of the place. I still had the cue in my hand, and as he chased me up the stairs, I turned around and threw it at him. I said that one day we — the Williams family — would own the goddamned pool hall. And we did.

43

But before we went into business, we had to do a whole lot of fighting — on the ice and in the streets, against ourselves and against the world. Craig Jordan, who was the best man at my wedding, once told me that he would do anything rather than pass our house on Bison Avenue and that a lot of kids felt the same way. We were a bunch of guys who wanted to run the show, and Jordan said that the only way he would come past our house was in his father's Saskatchewan Power truck. We fought locally and sometimes we'd travel to Regina. We didn't have any fear, but sometimes we'd get in over our heads, and once, a guy got stabbed.

One of the fiercest fights I ever had was with my brother Leonard. Our brother Hugh had a job putting up steel buildings for farmers and Leonard and I would do the labouring. One Friday night, Hugh told us not to leave the job before levelling a truck load of gravel that had arrived at 5:00 P.M.

Leonard was mad as hell. His fiancee was nursing in Saskatoon and he was impatient to be with her for the weekend. It didn't matter to me; I wasn't racing off to town. I was making $2.50 an hour, and I didn't want to waste my money. My plan was to stay out in the country and pick up a couple of jobs from the farmers. So Leonard was shovelling the gravel in some kind of frenzy. I was working as though I was on the payroll of the city of Vancouver. Leonard said, "If you don't start moving that gravel, I'll beat the crap out of you." I wasn't impressed and I didn't increase my pace. Suddenly Leonard whacked me with his shovel. The blow sent me flat on my back. Right where I fell was a steel thermos. I picked it up and threw it at him. It hit him in the head. For a little while, I thought I'd killed him.

There was always violence: in the pool hall, in the workplace, at a bar and on the ice. On one occasion, we brought my brother Morgan onto the bench of the Weyburn Midget team as a goaltender, because we knew there was going to be a donnybrook series with Estevan. He wasn't much of a goalie, but was very useful with his fists. We had played the first game in Estevan, and the fans had done their best to intimidate our goalie. There were these guys in their twenties yelling at him all the time and even spitting at him whenever they got the chance. They were put up to it by the Estevan coach, Punch McLean, who made a name for himself as a Junior coach by throwing garbage cans on the ice and getting involved in all

44

kinds of goonery. When I came off, McLean shouted at me, "Williams, I'm going to get someone to get you." I was fifteen years old at the time.

In the second game, in Weyburn, our plan was to intimidate Estevan's best player, a kid called Rod Flagginheim. He would never drop his gloves but he was a nice player. Morgan's job was to get the Flagginheim kid. His chance came when a fight erupted and the benches cleared. The problem was that in Weyburn we had a new director of recreation, and when he saw all this violence unfolding, he switched off all the lights. The arena was in total darkness. The fans started screaming for the lights, and most of the players were scared that they were going to get hammered in the darkness. Morgan and I were out on the ice with the idea of getting Flagginheim. I was next to Morgan and I said, "Can you see the Flagginheim kid?" But Morgan didn't have a scent. It turned out that the moment the lights went out, Flagginheim had crawled under a bench. It was a very smart move.

And there was the violence of the bars. My brother Trevor was sitting in a bar in Estevan one night when a guy came up to him and asked, "Are you Tiger Williams's brother?" Trevor said he was, and the guy punched him in the mouth, knocking some teeth out. Trevor called me on the phone, and he sounded quite sorry for himself. I told Trevor that he had to get the guy. I said he would get his chance and I didn't care what it took. He should do it even if he had to lift weights and take Kung Fu lessons. I said that in a place like Estevan he would get his opportunity. The guy would go off his guard, maybe get a little liquored up. Trevor should strike then. A few weeks later Trevor caught up with the guy and jumped him. He got plenty of revenge. A while after this incident, Trevor was sleeping in his trailer when he was awakened by gunshots. The guy had got himself a .30-30 Winchester and was shooting up the trailer. Trevor called me up again. This time my advice was that he should leave town.

At the age of sixteen, I realized that *I* had to leave town. I wasn't going to make it to the National Hockey League through the Weyburn hockey system, despite the support of someone like Jerry Murray. There were sixteen-year-olds from out of town playing Junior for the Weyburn Red Wings, but apparently there was no place for me. I was needed by the Midget team. This made me boil. I needed to be making clear progress through the ranks. I also had to earn some money. So I went to the oil patch.

I worked on the rigs, sometimes at temperatures of forty below. Jerry Manill, who sponsored the Weyburn Midget team, owned a service company, and he gave me the job, with hours that would enable me to play hockey from Friday to Sunday. I don't regret an hour I spent at the oil patch, though it was as hard as anybody could imagine, terribly cold, and dangerous. And a lot of your fellow workers were sad cases. I looked at their lives very closely. I felt sorry for them, because they seemed to be men without hope. They worked all day until five o'clock, then went to the bars and drank until closing time. And in the morning, they came in red-eyed, hung over. It was a depressing time for me because there was nobody at home, and there seemed to be a lot of emptiness in life. These guys worked so hard, and what did they have to show for it? They had money for the bars and the basics; beyond that, they didn't have a dime in their pockets. I would say to myself, "Hell, there has to be more in life than this."

The oil field was a hard education, but it was good one, too. I think it has always given me an edge over a lot of guys in professional hockey. I know what it is to come home from work with your back breaking; I know how hard most guys in the street have to work to make a living or to get a little extra for the wife and kids. Some young hockey players who come into the league today don't know what a full day's work does to your body and your mind.

When I was fifteen, I worked from midnight to 8:00 A.M. on a big D–8 *cat*, which was worth about $100,000 and was equipped with a big ripper that tore at the frost. In Saskatchewan in winter, there's eight feet of frost, and we had to rip through that to create a mudpit for drilling. If you were lucky, you would rip away six to eight inches at a time, then bulldoze it away and start again. Sometimes I think my back troubles probably go back to those nights on the big cat, tearing away at the prairie permafrost.

I did the work for Clarence Madsen and didn't always get paid, because Clarence was having a lean time. But that was no problem. Clarence had plenty of credit in my bank. When

46

things had been going well for him, he used to take me to baseball games and buy me cleats and the odd hockey stick. He was just a guy who liked sport and had a generous nature, and he must have thought I was quite a spirited kid. Certainly I loved the power of that cat. It was a big deal for a fifteen-year-old. I felt I was paying a little back to Clarence, and it also gave me the feeling that I was a big-time guy, somebody you could ask to do a job and know that it would be done. Clarence came out of his bad times and is now living well in Kelowna, British Columbia.

But in general that was a bad time for me, and it took a little while to come out of it. I had a lot of low moments, going home to the empty house in Bison Avenue. One night, after the oil patch I didn't go home. I went straight to a bar. I had my work clothes on, muddy boots, hard hat, and I stood at the bar and drank beer. After a few beers I started to have a real good time.

The trouble was that the place was beginning to fill up, and the management decided they didn't want this kid in his work clothes hanging around. They told me to leave. I was so bitter. I said that it had been fine to take my money when I was one of the few customers. Now they had plenty of business, they wanted to throw me out. I said there was no way they were going to get rid of me so easily. The people who ran the bar called the cops, but they couldn't get me out of there without a fight. I took on four barmen before the cops arrived. I was hauled off to jail, and I spent the night there. I remember thinking that my old schoolmates had a dance on that night, and there I was in the goddamned slammer. The management of the bar decided against laying charges or demanding payment for damages. They said that a lot of customers had enjoyed the fight; some even said they would have been prepared to pay an admission charge.

That kind of incident, I believe, stemmed mostly from my feeling that I wasn't really getting the kind of breaks I deserved. I put everything I had into hockey and still there were difficulties. And I could see that off the ice I had no kind of future at all. If I had any doubts about this, they were cleared away by a conversation I had with one of the workers at the oil patch. It was early in the morning, a terribly cold morning; his eyes were red and there was whisky on his breath and,

47

it seemed, a heavy weight on his shoulders. He told me to get out of the oil patch.

"Don't be like me," he said. "I've had my chances, but here I am going nowhere. Find something you can do and work at it. Maybe it's hockey or maybe it's school, but whatever it is, go to it now, don't wait around; because if you do, you'll wake up one morning and realize that it's all over. Don't wake up every goddamned morning of your life feeling miserable — and with not a dime to show for it."

It wasn't so much the words, as the way he said them. There was so much despair in his voice. His words have never left me. I swore then that I would devote everything to hockey. I would walk away from the oil patch and the beer drinking — at least, beer drinking during a hockey season.

I was fortunate to have coaches like Jerry Murray and Dwight McMillan in Bantam, Midget and Junior B hockey. Murray had told me about the value of effort and of always announcing yourself on the ice. He had done it in a very practical way — he had kept me on the team when everybody else wanted me off. McMillan reinforced the message and added some emphasis of his own. He was the best technical coach I had in minor hockey. He was also the strongest. Once he got mad at me when I shot a puck that deflected off a guy's stick, hit the roof and landed on his head. I apologized but it didn't do me any good. He punched me in the mouth. Apart from his knowledge of the game, his willingness to communicate with either his tongue or his fist, McMillan could point out very easily where your play was deficient and where you had to put in some extra work.

McMillan summed up his overall philosophy quite simply: "When you're losing, kill the bastards, so they will never do it again; and if you're winning, kill them just so they know what they're going to get next time." I saw how I could use some of that in my own game plan.

It was as though a lot of influences had come together and become one in my mind: my father, McMillan, Murray, the laughing faces of the kids when I spoke of my dreams, the whisky breath of the guy who said, "Run for it kid, while you still have a chance," and the sense that a lot of parents of kids I knew really didn't want me around — all of it fused as I worked at my hockey harder than ever before. The money would flow from the hockey, I decided. I might earn from the oil patch, but I would make no progress. There might be a thrill in the big machinery, but it would never be my machinery. I would be breaking my back on another guy's big cat. So now it would all have to change. I had to strip my life down to its essentials. I wouldn't have time for anything that didn't directly benefit my hockey. Every morning I went to the rink, and if I couldn't get ice time, I'd return to the house on Bison Avenue, go down to the basement and shoot the puck. Endlessly, I would fire the puck.

When I was sixteen, I played really well in the big Western Midget tournament in Swift Current. My team, the Weyburn Beavers, won the championship that spring, beating a Moose Jaw team that had Clark Gillies and Ed Staniowski. We won 6–5 in overtime, and I was hardly off the ice. I played defence, and though I wasn't very good skating backwards, the presence of my stick kept a lot of guys away. I was able to seal up the middle quite well. The following year, we returned to Swift Current as champions and got involved in a riot with Flin Flon. The guys from Flin Flon were playing it tough, and we decided to show them what some prairie boys could do. The officials lost control, and parents had to come onto the ice to break up the fighting.

By this time I had built up some frustration with the officials of Weyburn minor hockey. It seemed to me that the players didn't really matter. The important thing was for the Weyburn hockey program to look good, for trophies to be won. The fact that an individual might be ready to move up didn't matter so much as the strength of the Midget team. I felt that if I did make good, I would have a few individuals to thank. I would be in the debt of the guys who drove the team buses, and trainers and the coaches, who did it because it was in their blood, especially coaches who recognized that there would always be more to a successful hockey player than electric skates and nifty stickhandling. My whole future depended on that kind of perception and people who had the insight to make it. I had made all the commitments I could, fought in every available fight, and what I had to wait for was recognition.

Nobody had to tell me that I wasn't a Lafleur or a Bobby Orr, but I had proved something to myself in the years since I had first stepped onto the frozen Souris River. I had moved up

49

through all the levels, had played with faster, stronger, older kids — and no one had ever gotten the better of me. Someone might beat me once, but they couldn't come back and keep doing it. It may have been that some guys were going at three quarter speed while I was going at a hundred percent capacity with my legs on fire — and that was just to keep up. But a lot of guys couldn't do this. A lot of guys couldn't operate when they began to hurt, but it was never a problem for me.

I would do whatever was required to get out of Weyburn, to travel east beyond Winnipeg, west to the coast. Fortunately, Stan Dunn recognized this. Stan Dunn offered me a ticket. And I tore at his hand.

5

Stan Dunn was coach of the Swift Current Broncos, a languishing Junior club in the Western Canada Hockey League. Dark-haired, square-jawed, he was a classic hockey figure. He was about as sentimental as a monkey wrench, but be prided himself on an eye for character. He alone of the coaches in the Western Hockey League was ready to give Williams his head at that level of play where the NHL scouts made the life-changing decisions, where they picked out the winners from the multitude of contenders who glided and shot, punched and scuffled their way through the winter.

Dunn had never made it to the NHL but he had played and fought with many who had, and in Williams he believed that he saw an authentic pro. It is an instinct that comes with the years. Dunn played minor hockey in Rosetown, Saskatchewan. In 1947 he tried out for the Medicine Hat Tigers but was farmed out to Swift Current, popularly known as "Speedy Creek" in the dressing rooms of the WCHL. Briefly, he had spells with the Lethbridge Native Sons and Baltimore, and then three years with Lloydminster in Alberta. After a year in Scotland, he returned to Lloydminster, where he was involved in the minor hockey program. In 1971 he landed the Swift Current job, which on the face of it was no call to glory. But for Dunn it was the apex of his career as a hockey man. He took his wife, Sheila, and seven children to the town of sixteen

51

thousand and performed the remarkable task of turning around the Broncos. He was tough with the players and he panned carefully for the right kind of talent. Very quickly he found gold. He had Terry Ruskowski, who was to become an excellent pro; the right winger Don Larway, who would be a first round draft pick by Boston; and a prodigious young Métis named Bryan Trottier. And there was this outrageous kid from Weyburn, Tiger Williams. The jury was out on the controversial Williams, but Dunn had already reached his verdict. Dunn had decided that Williams had exactly those qualities of commitment and aggression that are essential for shaping a winning club.

For Williams, Dunn's decision was a deliverance from months of uncertainty and thousands of miles of fruitless travel. Because of his frustrations with the Weyburn hockey establishment, Williams had called Jack Shupe, the uncle of a boyhood rival, who was coaching in Medicine Hat, to see if he could find him a place in the Junior game. Medicine Hat had a Junior B affiliate in Vernon, B.C., and Shupe arranged for Williams to try out in Vernon. It was a doomed mission. Williams kicked his heels in B.C., waiting in vain for an inter-branch transfer from the hockey authorities in Saskatchewan. Without this clearance, he could not play for a team in another province. Earlier he had been similarly disappointed after spending some time in Humboldt, Saskatchewan, where the club had said that Williams must attend school. Williams had already made a final statement about formal education.

He had returned to Weyburn and settled for another year of Midget under the fierce coaching of Dwight McMillan. It was disappointing because in earlier years he had been encouraged to believe that he would always be in demand. As a Bantam he had never been short of offers to travel to hamlet teams and play in tournaments as a "guest." He would receive a few dollars and a sense of growing celebrity. In his oil patch days, he had been plucked away from the discomforts by the Bold family, who ran a Midget team in Fillmore, Saskatchewan. He used to spend the weekend with the Bolds, and he was dazzled by their resources. The Bolds had colour television and wall-to-wall carpeting. They even owned a skidoo. Moreover, they gave him a sense that he was wanted.

Dunn, though, performed a much more dramatic restoration of confidence. He said that he thought Williams could make it all the way to the NHL — in the process earning the Broncos $30,000 from the drafting club. Williams reported to the Swift Current training camp in 1971 in a mood of thinly disguised euphoria. He had cycled the 210

52

miles from Weyburn to Swift Current, nosing into a fierce headwind. A few weeks earlier, he had cycled from Saskatoon to Brandon to pick up a pair of made-to-measure skates. He was physically exhausted when he arrived in camp but was still eager to start his Junior career.

Right from the start, Stan Dunn looked after me. He got me a job on the pipeline and took me around to his house and said, "You'll stay here." He had a big family and he wasn't on a lot of money, but we both knew the situation. I might prove to be a burden on his butt. Or I might turn out to be a good investment. The good thing was that he was honest. He didn't wrap anything up. He knew my old man, he knew what kind of a financial lift it would be for my family if I made it into the big league. And, of course, the Broncos would make a big profit, too. It was all up front. Everybody knew what was involved, and if I ever let my responsibilities slip, he would remind me.

As a club, Swift Current's immediate priority was not shaping up kids like me for the draft three years down the road. They wanted guys eighteen or nineteen years old, who could go out on the ice and do the business right then. But Dunn was prepared to make the gamble. He played me all the time, whether I was good, bad or indifferent. He reckoned he would get it all back in my last year.

All Dunn ever insisted on from me or any of his other players was that we never skimp anything on the ice. If he had a major flaw as a coach, it may have been that he expected too much at practice. At times, you feared he was over-practising you, maybe running the risk of wearing you out. One night we put in a very stale performance and lost badly. The serious thing was that we had given up. Dunn came into the dressing room at the end of the game and said. "Nobody take their equipment off." Then he walked out. Eventually he returned, saying, "Okay, just take your skates off and put your shoes on." Some of us — including Trottier and me — had cowboy boots, and we just couldn't get them on over the equipment. We pulled on as many socks as we could and joined the others on the ice. Dunn had us working for at least two hours. It was one of the toughest physical experiences of my life. Guys were sliding around on their shoes and socks. We didn't get a break. He didn't say much. He just had us there, right at our limits. Some guys were ready to pass out when he finally dismissed us.

53

Then he came into the dressing room and said, "Never do that again."

Technically, Stan Dunn wasn't a great coach. His strength was in understanding guys, selecting the ones who had the stuff he needed when the going was tough. Also, he had a knack of conveying to you the need to be positive, of never holding back.

In a game against the Edmonton Oil Kings he was troubled that Phil Russell had given one of our players a heavy beating. He turned to me — it was in my first year — and said, "You know, we really shouldn't let Russell get away with that." Just as Dunn was saying this, Russell came skating by our bench on a rush. I just reached out and let Russell have it. Bang! I really whomped the guy. Russell went down like a sack. It looked like a guy racing through somebody's yard and getting hooked in the clothesline. I weighed about 160 pounds and Russell was 190 or so and about three inches taller.

Dunn realized I was a little radical in my thinking, so he never gave me the captaincy, never gave me public authority. But I think he wanted me to oversee things, be a strong influence. In the first couple of years, I gave him some problems. I was very wild on the ice, got a lot of suspensions and penalties. But he watched his investment very carefully, and I never had the suspicion that he was about to give up on me. In fact, it was usually the opposite feeling. He supervised every phase of my life. When my first year was over, he didn't want me to go back to Weyburn. He knew all about the Williams boys, how they terrorized the countryside. He wanted me to stay safely in Swift Current, where he could keep a close eye on everything I did.

Eventually he would monitor my courting of Brenda, my first Swift Current "steady," who would quickly be my wife. I knew right away that Brenda was the right girl for me, mentally, physically. She was everything I wanted, but Stan Dunn, of course, had his reservations. This was no reflection on Brenda, only her gender.

As far as Dunn was concerned, girls were bad news for hockey players, period. According to Dunn, part of the problem with broads was that they had parents, parents who said things like, "Oh, you might not make it in hockey, maybe you ought to go to university," and that might set a guy thinking, might take the edge off his game. Dunn was terrified of this happening to his better prospects.

When I was eighteen, he said to me, "Keep away from three things: wine, women and song, and I don't give a damn in which order." I guess Stan had seen a lot of guys who were going well, then got caught up with broads, and finished up just thinking about the broads. He needn't have worried about me because I always made it clear that nothing would come before my hockey.

But then I was eighteen, I was getting to be an old man, and I'd never had a steady broad. So I decided I had to find myself a lady. I went up to the school and did a little surveying. One thing I was sure about was that I didn't want to get hooked up with the kind of girl who hangs around the hockey rink. I wanted to meet an outsider. Some guys said that they wanted me to meet a friend, someone who was babysitting just across from the school. Her name was Brenda Dyck. She made a very good impression on me, but the trouble was she was very popular, had a lot of friends, and right away I had to weed them out.

Brenda was very good for me. I used to like her family life. It was always quiet in her house. There was nice carpeting. Before she met me, she didn't know that hockey existed. She was one of five sisters. There were no sons in the house. Her father didn't give a damn about hockey, had never played, never went to the games. It was a new experience for me, being around people who didn't care anything for hockey. But I liked the feel of it.

I introduced her to all the guys on the team but we didn't socialize much. I wanted to keep my private life separate from the hockey. There was also the problem of money. Neither of us had any money, or even a car. I got forty bucks a month. It could be quite tough, because a broad might want you to take her out, say to an A & W for a hamburger and a drink, and on forty bucks a month that wasn't always possible. But Brenda was very good. She didn't put any pressure on me, and I always told her that it would be different when I was drafted by the NHL. Then, we would take a few trips into the fast lane.

I never consciously thought that I would need a wife who could accept the demands of being married to a big-time hockey player. Maybe Brenda realized that hockey was so much a central part of my life that she just adjusted naturally. I never once put our relationship ahead of hockey, not even in that first stage of courtship. I told her that there was no chance we'd stay up late goofing around the night before a game. In my draft year, we went to a New Year's party on Monday night. At midnight, I said, "That's it, Brenda, I'll be going home to bed," and she said, "You can't, it's New Year's Eve." I told her that I didn't give a damn what night it was, I had a game on Tuesday.

During the season we had a curfew set at midnight. Some nights, I would be at Brenda's house and Stan Dunn would pull up around eleven o'clock, flash his lights, beep the horn. Once Brenda thought it was some guys coming around to take us to a party. It was Stan, sitting in the dark, keeping a night eye open on his investment. Once he fined me twenty bucks for being late, and that was a cruel blow. I steamed into him, said, "Why are you always picking on me, you bastard?" He never said why he paid such close attention and it's really only now that I see he was desperate for me to make it.

Also, I guess, it was very easy for a kid to lose his way in Junior hockey. You spent so much time on the bus, "the iron lung." I recall one trip out to the coast. We played seven games in ten nights. Our last game was in Victoria. The trainer, Dick Abel, also drove the bus, and when he got drunk in Victoria, I had to drive the bus off the ferry. Stan Dunn had walked off the ferry talking to a scout named Harvey Roy. I was one of the few guys on the team who knew how to drive a bus. After the big cat it was nothing, of course.

Stan Dunn's major challenge was to keep a bunch of young men centring their thinking on hockey. You had so much time to kill on the bus, to think, "Do I really need this?" We would get to a rink at 6:45 PM for an eight o'clock game, having bused five hundred miles straight and having last eaten at midday. If we were lucky, we'd had a steak sandwich at Joe's truck stop. Dunn would come into the dressing room and say, "I don't give a shit how tired you are, there are scouts out there. Johnny Bower is out there with Torchy Schell." He would always throw in names like Bower, the great hero, and Schell, the ace scout for the Maple Leafs. It was like putting smelling salts under a guy's nose, and it wasn't that dishonest, because one night Torchy Schell arrived in a building to look at me, and it was just as well that I always played as though the whole frigging National Hockey League was in whichever rinky-dink little place I happened to be working.

Brenda realized how hard it was early in our relationship. I went off on a trip with the team for back-to-back games in Flin Flon, then the big swing down to Winnipeg, six or seven hundred miles away. After the second game in Flin Flon, we just grabbed some Kentucky Fried Chicken and hit the road. You have to know that northern Manitoba country to appreciate how cold it was that night, and just an hour or so out of Flin Flon I got an attack of diarrhea. Every ten minutes we had to stop the bus so I could relieve myself. I was also vomiting. And then there was the cold. We got to a little town called The Pas and looked for a doctor or the guy who ran the drugstore. We couldn't find either so we just pushed on.

When we got to the town of Dauphin, I told Dunn I just couldn't go on. I was losing control of my body, and we still had a couple of hundred miles to go. We had a game scheduled for Monday night in Winnipeg. We booked into this little hotel, which had one wash basin to every floor. Another guy, Stewie McLellan, had also gone down with food poisoning, and we just took our blankets and pillows to the toilet, which was unheated. At dawn we raised a druggist, threw some stuff down, and moved off.

When we checked into a motel in Winnipeg I went straight to bed. I felt as though I was dying. I asked my roommate, Ronnie Delorme, to get me some jello, which was about the only thing I could imagine getting down and keeping down. Around six thirty, I was lying in the darkened room feeling weaker than I'd ever felt in my life, when I heard the bus revving up outside. The old iron lung was trundling off to another game.

Suddenly the door swung open and Stan Dunn came marching into the room. "What the hell do you think you're doing?" he said. "Get your goddamned clothes on. We have a game tonight." I couldn't believe it. I just looked at him. I guess my expression was blank. He added, "I don't give a shit how you feel. Get your clothes on. We're going."

I went to the rink and I played. And I scored three goals. Right after the game, we climbed on the bus and drove to Swift

Current, another five hundred miles. We got back to town at about eight o'clock in the morning. Brenda was waiting, and so were my landlord and landlady, Gord and Millie Allsen. Really, they were great friends. Gord was the administrator at the Swift Current hospital and he was the first man to give me any idea of business, of how to handle money and make it work. When he saw my face, he said, "Holy shit, what's wrong with you?" My cheeks were sunken and there were black rims around my eyes. Gord drove me straight to the hospital. He had me checked out for a virus or something more serious. But really, I told him, it was just how it was in Junior hockey — how it was with a coach like Stan Dunn.

I told Brenda that it wasn't going to get any easier. In fact, in some ways it would get worse. The higher you went, the more pressure there was. To this day I've never relented. I put hockey first then and now, because I've always known it would pay for the clothes on my kids' backs; I knew that if I put everything into it, I would get something back.

I could never forget the time when I was young and some guy called at our house just before Christmas and left some presents for all us kids, and then later I learned that we were on some kind of list. That was something that would always keep my afterburner glowing. I explained all of this to Brenda when I made the hard decisions about not staying out at night when we felt like having a good time; and it was hard, because when you're young, it's natural to want to have a good time.

But, really, when you thought about it, there was no problem. You had to do something that would change your life and maybe help the rest of your family. You had to work at levelling the odds against you.

So I told Brenda about the ways of hockey from the moment I met her. And she groomed me in matters beyond the rink. I guess that's the most valuable exchange of my life. Brenda taught me that some very important things existed outside hockey and she accepted my point that, as long as I played the game professionally, it had to be my top priority for the sake of our future. With Brenda's help, I've never had any difficulty drawing the line between the needs of life and my dedication as a hockey player. I know how lucky I was to get a girl like her. And, I suppose, a coach like Stan Dunn.

6

J unior hockey was as hard as Williams could ever have imagined but at no time did he suspect that it would prove too hard. Coach Dunn quickly concluded that Williams had enough of the right stuff to make his investment safe. For Williams the rewards far outstripped the difficulties. The chief reward was not the forty dollars a month pocket money he got from the Swift Current Broncos, but something else — the chance to prove to the world that he was capable of playing professional hockey. This was the prize he had sought for so long.

Williams also received another reward, one that he had not sought, had not expected. He got the chance to observe and make vital contributions to the early phase of the career of a player he would eventually come to consider one of the two or three outstanding hockey players of his generation: Bryan Trottier. Trottier and Williams became close friends. Trottier, two years younger, looked up to Williams as a tough, more experienced player who was prepared to spend time helping junior teammates. Williams was impressed by the kid's extraordinary talent and he was determined to protect that talent as fiercely as he could. Williams frequently spent weekends with the Trottiers, a Métis family who lived in Val Marie, Saskatchewan. At the end of their Junior careers, the two friends were drafted into the NHL in 1974.

59

The friendship stretched beyond Junior days. On one summer visit, when Trottier was an established star with the Islanders and Tiger Williams was a big name in Toronto, Williams was helping Trottier with the day's work, which was the castration of calves. The two men took the calves' testicles back to the farmhouse and cooked a meal of Canadian "prairie oysters." Trottier's fiancée, who was also visiting, was appalled; she said that if they didn't stop, she would return home to New York immediately. They carried on with the meal, but the courtship survived: not long afterwards, Bryan Trottier was married quietly in a Swift Current registry office. Even through the violence and conflicts of the NHL Williams and Trottier remain close friends.

One of my big jobs in Swift Current was to look after this little guy on the team who played hockey as though it was the easiest, most natural thing in the world. His name was Bryan Trottier. Even then he was unbelievable. In practice you could never get the puck off the little bastard. He had so much balance, so much skill with his stick, and he skated like the wind.

What was natural for him was unnatural for me. A university professor explained it to me later. I don't have the proper leg structure to skate well. I have a long body and short legs, when I should have a short body and long legs. Furthermore, I'm not bow-legged. My knees come in where they should go out. That's why I'm not a gazelle on skates. It is not because I didn't work hard enough when I was a kid. If your skating developed with every hour you spent on the ice, I would have looked like Peggy Fleming by my tenth birthday.

It may sound funny now, that I was assigned to help Bryan Trottier, but then there really were things that I could teach him and things I could do for him. The first thing I had to teach him was not be be scared. He arrived in my second year, a sixteen-year-old whose eyes were wide-open at this big world. The apprehension showed on the ice. With any kind of time or space he looked brilliant. But when anyone took a run at him, he jumped or ducked. Stan Dunn gave the problem a little thought and decided to put Trottier on a line between me and a guy called Brian (Barney) Back. Barney was a tough guy; he had been playing Junior hockey since he was fourteen years old, and he could throw a tremendous check. As a bonus, he also had a good shot. Dunn said that if people bothered Trottier, we had to run at them like trains. After a game or two, you

60

could see Trottier's confidence growing. He was getting a little more room to operate, wasn't taking so many hard hits or getting blind-sided so often. Dunn also had us playing mind games with Trottier. Before a tough game Dunn would say to one of us, "Warn the kid that it could be hard tonight, that he might have to take a check or two — set him up mentally."

Terry Ruskowski was a very good junior, very mature, and he and Barney and I would sit around talking about how we were going to help the kid. We would say to him, "Look, you're going to have to take a check, and the thing to learn is that it is never going to hurt you as much as you sometimes might imagine." It was something that needed a lot of care, because in the course of a season in Junior hockey you would see some great players, but a lot of them never got over their first fears. However good a kid was, if he got shy of the boards, he was always going to struggle in the big league. And there was one thing you couldn't soften or disguise: the game at Junior level could be brutally hard, and for a kid who thought the game was only about wrist shots and deking and great skating, reality could arrive like a fist in the throat.

How hard was it? Lou Klashinski was a trainer in Weyburn when I was a stick boy. He moved to Medicine Hat, where they had a very tough Junior team featuring the Gassoff boys, Bob, Kenny, and Brad. Klashinski used to sneak over from the Medicine Hat dressing room and tape my right hand, so that when I hit a guy it was like a cement glove. Klashinski knew that the Medicine Hat guys would be gunning for me. One night, after Lou had taped my hand, I had a series of fights with the entire Gassoff family. How hard was it? In another game, Bob Gassoff took a penalty in the first minute. He skated up to the referee and said, "You give me another goddamned penalty and I'll break your ankle." Two minutes later Gassoff returned to the ice and when he immediately drew a penalty, he just two-handed the referee and did break his ankle. He got suspended for a few games. Nobody made much of a fuss. If you didn't like it hard, you just got out of Junior hockey. Junior hockey was a jungle where the animals were fighting for their lives and nowhere was tougher than Flin Flon.

Flin Flon was where you found out about yourself as a hockey player. If you didn't get scared in Flin Fon, you could

61

be pretty sure you were going to be okay. To be honest, I rather enjoyed the place.

I used to start psyching myself up when the old iron lung got within five hundred miles of Flin Flon. There was no point in going into that town and waiting for things to happen. You had to impose yourself upon events. Walking into the rink, you'd get heckled; some of the fans, liquored up, would try to make trouble. They'd say things like, "You get near the boards and we'll knock your teeth out." But you'd just walk through them contemptuously. It was a small rink, and it was always a grinding game. There were screens behind the goaltenders but not along the sides, so if a Flin Flon player didn't get you with a stick or a fist, the chances were that a fan would. They were the meanest, ugliest-spirited fans in all of Canada.

In one game, one of our players, Kelly Pratt, was being baited and he said to me, "See that guy over there, the next time the puck goes over there I'm going to pretend to hit somebody but I'm going to cross-check him and knock every goddamned tooth out of his head." The situation developed perfectly. A Flin Flon player came down the boards and Pratt reached out to check him. The guy ducked, the man behind him ducked, and Pratt hit a teenage girl right in the mouth. The Flin Flon crowd was bitter then. A lot of teams lost there because situations slipped so easily out of control.

Flin Flon had always had good players, people like Bobby Clarke and Reggie Leach, but even the bad players believed they were good playing in that atmosphere. Take old Jack McIlhargey. He wouldn't have made Junior, let alone the National Hockey League, if he hadn't played at Flin Flon. But in that little arena up there he sometimes resembled Bobby Orr. I know that some teams were absolutely petrified by the idea of playing there. But we had a good record against them; it was as though they brought out the best in us. I know I used to prowl outside the dressing rooms before a game, just daring somebody to say something provocative.

For me, I suppose it was kind of a rehearsal for the trips to Philadelphia, when I would declare to the toughest, meanest characters in the NHL that I was ready to fight anyone. Flin Flon, like the Spectrum in Philly, was simply a challenge that had to be met. The club had a reputation for manufacturing

62

tough players, and their coach, Paddy Ginnell, didn't think there was any line to be drawn in the pursuit of success. Ginnell put some players in the NHL, but I believe he also destroyed a lot by his attitude. I've tried to explain my own feelings about violence, how it troubles me when I'm involved in an incident with a guy who I know isn't capable of returning the favour. When you're young, you might do that kind of thing, as we tried to do that time with the Flagginheim kid. But violence was Ginnell's basic tactic. He would bring up guys just for one game, guys whose sole job was to beat the crap out of your best player. I'm glad that I've never been in a situation that clear-cut, that none of my coaches ever came to me and said specifically, "Do in so-and-so."

In my final year in Junior, Stan Dunn told the team, "Look, we've got guys like Williams and Ruskowski who are in their draft year and it's really important that we have a good playoff. The Eastern scouts only pay attention to the playoffs."

It gives me a lot of satisfaction that I probably nailed down my place in the NHL on the strength of performances against Flin Flon in the playoffs.

My challenge that final year was simple. I had to knock in 50 or more goals during the season, and then go out of the year with a bang. I achieved both objectives, though the first target looked doubtful as early as November, when Clark Gillies sent me flying through a screen at Regina. Gillies hit me with a good check and my hand went through the mesh. Gillies, who was already a big man, had all his weight on me, and I was just hanging there by my thumb. A doctor in Swift Current said that I had broken the thumb and he put on a cast. In my draft year I felt I had to be sure of everything concerning my body — and so I got a friend to fly me to Regina. There, a doctor who treated the Roughriders football players confirmed the original diagnosis. The cast was made of fibreglass and became a very effective weapon.

A lot of guys claimed that I wore the cast long after it was necessary, and that eventually I used to take it off between games and then put it on before going on the ice, like an enforcer with a knuckleduster. But it wasn't true. The injury and the cast made it difficult for me to hold the stick with anything like a controlled grip, and because of this my goals rate lagged in the first half of the year. This created a lot of tension in me. I had to draw attention to myself and then deliver in the fire of the playoffs. But then the fibreglass cast did have its benefits, and quite a few guys felt its force. Cam Connor, the tough guy and goalscorer of Flin Flon, was one who really suffered. We got involved in a big fight, and I just started hitting him over the head, as though I had a hammer in my hand. I gave him three hard whops and that was just about the end of him.

We beat Flin Flon in that series with a goal by Barney Back in overtime of the final game. It had been a war all the way. We split the first two games in Flin Flon, and they won the third in Swift Current, when I didn't play, because of an injury. So we had to go back to Flin Flon, back to the goddamned company town where the mine laid on hockey to keep the workers happy. I suppose it was like the way they kept the workers happy in Ancient Rome, when they'd just throw a few Christians to the lions. Here, it was a case of throwing in a few hockey players. The problem for Flin Flon, though, was that we weren't prepared to be mauled to death. It was the first time Swift Current had won a series against Flin Flon, the first time a team had consistently gone into their building and really challenged the players — and the fans as well. Back's winner was a beauty. He really drilled it. The Williams-Trottier-Back line showed up well all night.

In the NHL draft later that year, the New York Islanders took Trottier, Toronto took me, and Barney Back never made it. It was a pity. He was a really good friend but I guess deep down he didn't want it enough. He wasn't always in the best of shape. Maybe he had been too long in Junior, had absorbed too much punishment and endured too much pressure. He had been playing Junior since the age of fourteen; that was a lifetime of taking on bigger guys, fighting to establish yourself. Maybe he didn't have the hunger that drove on people like Trottier, Ruskowski, and me. Ruskowski was drafted in the fourth round by Chicago but he had already signed for Houston Aeros of the World Hockey Association.

Naturally, after we knocked out Flin Flon, Stan Dunn pushed his point about the value of playoff hockey to the draft. In the next round, we met Regina, a team that had some excellent players, particularly Gillies, Dennis Sobchuk — a centre who had already signed in the WHA — and Eddie Staniowski in goal. All these players had learned their business, and they were able to beat us out, largely because of goaltending. Staniowski was very solid, and we had a sixteen-year-old guarding our net; that was the difference. Regina went on to the Memorial Cup, where they played the St. Catharines Black Hawks, Bobby Hull's old team.

Wilf Paiement played for St. Catharines in the final, did well and got drafted in the first round. California Seals picked a defenceman named Rick Hampton from the Black Hawks and paid very big bucks. Greg Joly, a defenceman from Regina Pats, went to Washington. Both of these defencemen — one the first player picked in the whole draft, the other the third pick overall — were real flops when they got into big league hockey, but they looked terrific in the Memorial Cup.

To me, this proved Stan's point, and it also underlined the fact that the whole game was a bit of a lottery. You could play your guts out in all those rinky-dink games in all those little arenas across the prairie, but all the effort could be wiped away if you weren't quite right for the playoffs, if you had an injury or some problem and the big-shot scouts from the East caught you on a bad night.

It also shows how much ego comes into play. Some scout, a little guy who knows his hockey, can watch a kid all year, watch him playing hurt, or when he has the flu or the toothache or food poisoning picked up at some truck stop on a long bus trip, and this little scout can say, "Hey, I know the kid is good; I know his habits, his approach to the game — he always comes to play." And the big guy can say, "No, I didn't see it tonight," and that could be the whole goddamned ball game.

It's scary to think how much hard work, how many hopes, could have gone down the tube for me if I'd gotten a bad injury, if I'd let that broken thumb keep me off the ice and spoil my rhythm in that last year in Junior, that last year when all the money was on the table.

But for me the money had been there all the time, really. In one way or another it had always been on the table. The ambition to make it had been put there by so many people. By old McCarthy rationing his television set. By all the guys who laughed at me when I made my claims. By old Henry Yeik chasing me out of the pool hall. By all my brothers, raising hell, wanting to run the show, some goddamned show, somewhere. Most of all, by my old man.

What Stan Dunn did was keep me focussed. He prodded me when he thought I might just be wavering a little. He didn't have to do too much prodding.

I married Brenda just a few days before the NHL draft. We didn't have any money but I told her there was nothing to worry about; I'd get drafted high, and we'd have a hell of a honeymoon.

7

It was a honeymoon composed of the dreams of a prairie boy. It took David and Brenda, and Herb Pinder, Jr., to Toronto and Cincinnati and Chicago. At every city stop, the red carpet was rolled out to this young couple who had never before travelled east of Winnipeg. In Toronto King Clancy showed them around and he gave David cufflinks inscribed with the insignia of the Toronto Maple Leafs. In Cincinatti Bill Dewatt, owner of the WHA Stingers, football's Bengals and baseball's Reds, said that he would make Tiger Williams "an offer he couldn't refuse," a joking reference to the catchphrase from the current movie "The Godfather." But there was no flippancy when Dewatt talked business with Pinder, who, apart from helping David and Brenda through the mysteries of exotic menus in famous restaurants, had the important task of negotiating the hockey player's first professional contract.

Pinder was from a wealthy Saskatoon family, and he was then in the process of graduating from the Harvard Business School. Today he is still moved by the memory of that trip with the young hockey player and his bride. It is not often that you see a young man embracing the reality of his dreams, dreams that had been scorned by others and then fashioned against overwhelming odds. If Pinder has an abiding memory of the trip, it is of Williams walking through Chicago's O'Hare Airport. He had on a huge cowboy hat and was waving his signing-bonus cheque. It was for $30,000, and by the time Williams returned to the prairie, it would be showing considerable wear. At the airport, it seemed to Pinder that the hockey player wanted to embrace the world. Pinder was reminded of the story of a teacher, impressed by Williams's showing in a technical aptitude test, who asked him to take it over as a check on startlingly good results. Williams had scrawled across the second test, "N-H-L."

"Tiger's life," says Pinder, "is formed by a series of concentric circles. At the centre, there is Tiger and his family, and then radiating out are hockey, friends, business contacts, and the world. Sometimes hockey supplants his family in the inner circle, because it may be a time he considers particularly crucial to his career. But the rest is rigid. At the age of nineteen or twenty he had shown an astonishing capacity to determine personal goals and then pursue them with great determination, great clarity.

"I was playing golf one day with an assistant pro in Saskatoon, who was from Swift Current. I was just beginning to get involved in pro sports, and I remarked that apparently they had some good prospects up in Swift Current, and he said, 'Yes, but the one who is a certainty to go all the way is Tiger Williams. Tiger is different. He has something you can't put your finger on but it works.'

"I made contact with Tiger, had some brief conversations with him. Once we chatted at an airport. Tiger had the fibreglass cast on his hand, and it was obviously giving him a lot of problems, but he said that nothing would prevent his scoring 50 goals. I went over to Swift Current for the game in which he got number 50. They were playing Brandon, and I noticed that the Brandon players gave Tiger quite a bit of room. When he scored the goal, he was just ecstatic. It was something to see."

Pinder's presence on the trip to the three cities, his official status as Williams's agent, is an extraordinary story in itself. Williams had come under strong pressure from the Swift Current Broncos to drop Pinder and sign up with one of the big eastern agents, Richard Sorkin of New York or Dave Schatia of Montreal. Sorkin flew into Swift Current to address the players, who were gathered together by the club. He made a haughty pitch. He said that the players would be foolish to put their hockey affairs in the hands of "little guys" in the West. What they needed was a big guy from the East, a guy who had the "in" with the owners and the league, a guy who knew how the whole business worked. Sorkin was such a man, he suggested.

Williams, mindful of the common belief that, as a matter of course, Junior clubs received kickbacks from favoured agents, listened to

Sorkin with a rising fury. The he rose to his feet and asked the man from New York, "What's my name?" Sorkin said that he didn't know the players personally, of course, but that wouldn't affect his ability to look after their affairs. Williams walked out of the room, despite being ordered by club officials to stay. Some years after this incident, Richard Sorkin was sentenced to two years' imprisonment for the misappropriation of clients' funds.

Herb Pinder was different. Pinder was of the prairies, he had a well-connected family and a solid financial background. And, vitally, he had taken the time to find out about Williams and his aspirations. But Pinder, for a brief time, had one serious rival. It was Schatia of Montreal. Schatia's approach was somewhat more subtle than that of Sorkin, and he did provide himself with an introduction to Williams that Pinder describes as "literally breath-taking." Through his good contacts within the NHL, Schatia was able to find out that Williams had been ranked highly by the league's central scouting staff. This ranking, and a detailed assessment of his ability, would be issued to each of the NHL clubs, virtually ensuring that Williams would go in the first round of the annual draft. (In fact, it was the first year of underage drafting, and Williams would be selected thirty-first overall, but in practical — that is, financial — terms, he would be regarded as a first-round pick.) Williams was intoxicated by the news and impressed by Schatia's ability to produce it.

Pinder recalls the weekend Schatia made his big move. "I was still at Harvard, and that weekend I had been away skiing. When I got back to my room at the college, the phone was ringing. Apparently it had been ringing off the wall all weekend. Tiger was on the line. He could hardly speak with excitement. Everything he had been working for, for so many years, had been achieved, and this guy Schatia had come up with the good news. Tiger said he wasn't so sure of our arrangement now. Maybe he needed some Eastern guy who knew his way around. I said that it was his decision, that he should weigh things carefully and do what he thought best. He said he would think about it. Apparently he did some research, checked me out a little. Then, twenty-four hours later, he called me back and said, 'There's no problem. You're my man.' "

I went with Herb Pinder for various reasons, but the basic one was that he wasn't like all the others. He didn't just tell me what I wanted to hear. In that last year in Junior, the phone never stopped. Every night there would be some agent from the East on the line saying something like, "Hi Dave, how many goals you got?" They never asked how I was feeling, what problems or maybe fears I had. They just had that bottom-line question about the number of goals I'd scored, and then they'd tell me what a wonderful job they were going to do for me. There would be so many rich pickings.

Sorkin from New York was like that. He arrived in Swift Current in a three-piece suit, and he was full of big promises. He said he knew what hockey players wanted. They wanted money and cars and broads, not necessarily in that order, and he was the man to provide all these things. I was sickened. I asked Sorkin if he knew my name. I was asking him what the hell he knew about my hopes and ambitions and what sacrifices I'd made to achieve them. Did he have any idea what it was like playing up in Flin Flon with a cast on your hand? Did he know what it was like on the iron lung sweating with fever, and then having to go play, knowing that you were weak and vulnerable to an injury or a bad beating. Did he know about that? Did he care about any of that? Or were we just commodities, young guys he could use to turn a quick profit?

I walked out of the room and told the other guys to follow me. I could tell that a lot of them wanted to come out with me, but none of them moved. You could see that they were scared of the situation. Bill Burton, the owner of the club, and Stan Dunn were in the room. They had made it clear that they wanted everyone to sign up with Sorkin. I told them that there was no way I was going to put my future in the hands of a guy who didn't even know my name.

Soon after the meeting with Sorkin we were due to play two games in Flin Flon. On the journey, Stan Dunn came to sit beside me. He said that I really ought to sign with Sorkin. It was what the club wanted, and it would prevent any possible selection problems. I said that the club could forget it. There wasn't any kind of pressure that could persuade me to sign up with Richard Sorkin. Well, the club applied the heaviest possible pressure. They didn't play me against Flin Flon in the first game, which we lost quite badly. After the game, I said to Dunn, "You better play me tomorrow night. If you don't, I'm going to call every goddamned newspaper in Western Canada and tell them the whole story." I played the following night; we won, and I didn't hear any more about who I should select as my agent.

I told Pinder that I was choosing him because he seemed like a smart enough guy, he had family on the board of the Royal Bank of Canada and, if anything went wrong, it wouldn't be such a long journey for me to go up to Saskatoon and throw bricks through the windows of his father's drugstores.

Pinder did a good job with the contract negotiations, and he was also a fine guide to the fast lane we travelled through Toronto and Cincinnati and Chicago. East of Winnipeg was a whole new world to Brenda and me. I had been to the West Coast with the Broncos, strutted around the foyers of hotels in New Westminster and Victoria saying to myself, "Boy, this is the big time," but the East was more mysterious, maybe a little more threatening. Down East, you thought, was where the hockey players were bigger and meaner and better, because there was something in their environment which made them that way. It was wonderful to make the trip and good to have a guy with Herb's class pointing out the things we didn't know, like the etiquette of five-star restaurants and how you tackle a bowl of baked onion soup, but the only surprise was in the details of it. I had always told Brenda that we would be making this trip. There hadn't been any doubt in my mind, other than the fear of serious injury, because I knew that I was mentally tough enough to do whatever was required.

The Maple Leafs put us up at the Westbury Hotel, close to Maple Leaf Gardens. King Clancy was very attentive. He took us horse racing and bought lavish meals, and it was clear from the first few seconds of our first meeting that we would hit it off. He loaned us his car — a Lincoln, which had the number plate MLG (Maple Leaf Gardens) 2. Ballard's car was identical except, of course, his was MLG-1. A lot of the negotiating was done in Clancy's office, where he had a fish tank filled with piranha. Every so often Clancy would throw some goldfish into the tank, and as the piranha tore at them, he would say, "That's how I like my hockey players — hungry."

Pinder knew that I felt a strong attachment to the Maple Leafs, and he was concerned that I would let my emotions show and perhaps weaken our bargaining position. He had warned me, "If Gregory (general manager Jim) or Clancy mention money to you, don't say anything. Just keep a blank expression."

So when Clancy suddenly said, "Tiger, we'll pay you $75,000 a year," I didn't say a word. I just got up from my chair and walked over to the fish tank. I watched the piranha darting around, and I said, "When I'm a pro, that's the way I'll be."

We were in Toronto for four days and having the best of times when Cincinnati called. We agreed to go down to Ohio to talk to them. There were more big dinners. I had Rockefeller oysters for the first time. I was beginning to feel like a Rockefeller myself. Cincinnati made a very good offer. They would pay me a $75,000 signing bonus and $100,000 a year for four years. "Jeez," I thought, "I can pick up nearly half a million dollars even if it turns out that I can't play the goddamned game as a pro." But there were some drawbacks. The rink in Cincinnati wouldn't be ready for another year, so I would have to go down to play in Phoenix, Arizona, and I couldn't really imagine playing hockey in the desert. And there was Toronto.

I put in a call to my dad, and he said that he wanted to see me in the NHL; he wanted to be able to turn on the television and see me play. This was a big factor, the feeling for family and for Canada. The goal had been the NHL. The extra money Cincinnati was offering would be some compensation for missing that goal, but I was far from certain it would be enough. Cincinnati wanted a decision and so did Toronto. The Maple Leafs asked me to return to Toronto, but I said that I would prefer a neutral city. Cincinnati gave Herb Pinder some money for expenses, as did Toronto, and we flew to Chicago.

We stayed on the top floor of the Palmer House Hotel on Michigan Avenue. It was wonderful up there amid the skyscrapers, the city and the lakeshore glittering so far below. However much I had planned for this, anticipated it, I was still a prairie kid. I dropped a glass from a window to see the effect when it struck the sidewalk; I told Brenda it was all right to drop a glass there, because nobody went down a back street in Chicago at night. The glass was pulverized; it broke into a million pieces. Unlike the glass, I was indestructible. This was the greatest of times.

The more I thought about it, the more obvious it became that Toronto would be my choice. There was the emotion of it and also the practical possibilities. The Maple Leafs needed help on the left side. Errol Thompson would later prove him-

72

self a scorer in the NHL, but he wasn't yet in top form, and Garry Monahan was also struggling. Neither of them had scored more than 9 goals the year before, and I said to Pinder that if I couldn't score 9 goals in a season just off my helmet, we'd better forget it. And there was something else, something that I realized was playing on King Clancy's mind. The Maple Leafs didn't have any tough guys. There was a vacuum to fill within the club and with the fans and the media. Whatever else the Maple Leafs needed, they had to have some heart, someone who was ready to stand and fight. I had been doing it all my life, on and off the ice. I had the perfect training, and I think that King Clancy recognized this right away.

Herb Pinder had negotiated a deal with Toronto that wouldn't have as much emphasis on the front end as the Cincinnati offer. The Toronto proposal was to pay me a $30,000 signing bonus, $100,000 the first year ($65,000 if I went to the minors) and guaranteed salaries of $110,000 and $115,000 in my second and third years. I would have another $115,000 guaranteed in my option year. Pinder advised me that the structure of the Toronto contract would be easier on tax and would also put me at a higher level when it came to negotiations on a new contract.

Whatever happened, the Leafs were committed to paying me $435,000. I thought of that bottom line and balanced the guaranteed extra money from Cincinnati against the fact that I would be operating down in the desert, so far from places like the Forum in Montreal, Madison Square Garden, Boston Garden and Chicago Stadium. These places were hockey. Phoenix was nowhere. I wanted to hear the sound of the big crowds, follow those guys whose pictures I had collected back in Saskatchewan. And I thought of the pride my dad and my brothers would have watching me play on television, and the way I would feel them with me when I played. It was a very important factor for me, and the more I thought about it, the more convinced I became. I said to Herb Pinder, "I think we'd better phone Toronto and tell them I'm coming."

King Clancy and Johnny McLellan flew into Chicago, and we all met in the big restaurant at O'Hare Airport. Over the meal I signed the contract. A waiter took a photograph. I said to King Clancy, "Tell Harold Ballard he won't regret a cent. I'll do a real job for him and I'll kick the shit out of anyone who gets in my way." We shook hands, and I told Clancy I would see him in the fall, when I would be ready.

Herb Pinder joined Brenda and me on the flight back to Canada. We arrived in Winnipeg, which used to be the eastern boundary of my world, and I thanked Herb for being a good agent and a good friend, and for giving me all the scoops on the fast life.

Brenda and I would have the summer of our lives. I don't think I'd ever realized someone could be so happy. But before we had our summer, I had to go back to Weyburn. I had to see my father and do a few things I had always promised myself, back when I used to get thrown out of the pool hall and have to wait at the drugstore for my friends, browsing through the paperback rack and not having the price of a goddamned soda. I was going to do something I had vowed to do when I used to have to beg for a loan of a hundred dollars from the bank and collect bottles to earn a buck or two.

First, I went to the bank in Weyburn to cash my signing-bonus cheque. I said that I wanted the money in $10 bills. The cashier said that they didn't have enough $10 bills. I said there was no problem: I would wait. I guess it was a little like having a winning hand in a big game of poker. You want to enjoy the moment. Eventually they handed me over a big pile of $10 bills. I counted them out, and then I went over to the pool hall, the pool hall I had been kicked out of so many times.

I had always vowed that when I made it to the NHL, I would come back to the town and the pool hall and say, "Look, I told you I'd make it. Here is the evidence. You laughed at me when I didn't have the price of a soda pop. Now laugh at me when I can buy the whole goddamned place for cash."

But when the moment came, it wasn't quite as I'd imagined. The guys who had laughed hardest at me, the guys I really wanted to see my gesture, weren't around. But there were some guys in the place, and if some of them didn't give a damn about me and my money, I knew some did, and I knew the word would go around. It seems a bit strange now, but I was twenty years old and had a lot of bitterness in me. And what's the point of winning something if you can't enjoy the victory? My enjoyment then was producing the evidence that people

74

had been wrong about me all the time. Really, I had been going somewhere. Anyway, I counted out the money on the little bar in the pool hall, and I said, "Thirty grand from the Maple Leafs — not bad, eh?"

It was time to see my father. Of course, he was proud and delighted. He was moving into a new house, and I asked him what he wanted. He said he was fine, he had everything he needed. So I went out to buy him a Lazy Boy recliner, but I said that I would have him come to stay with me in Toronto, and then I would take him out to look at some rare stamps. My dad always had a passion for stamps, and if he ever had some spare cash — which was rare enough — he'd put it aside to buy a stamp. I said I'd get him some damned fine stamps, and he said that would be good. Down the road, I knew I'd be able to help my family, would be able to build up a rainy-day fund, but I had to make my money work. I had a bride and I had responsibilities, and $30,000 was only the down payment on my career. I wanted to get my dad the luxury of fine stamps because all our lives had been about getting by, about rounding up enough cash to get the basics of life. I wanted some of that first real money of my life to go on something that wasn't simply material. Rare stamps were luxuries beyond a working man who had fought to bring up eight kids. I wanted to change that a little.

I also wanted to enjoy myself. I felt it was time to drink a little beer. I took Dick Abel, the trainer of the Swift Current Broncos, out on the town. I said, "Look, pal, you've been good to me, I'm going to take you out and I'm paying the shot." We went up to the beer parlour, drank a terrible amount of beer, then went to a diner. We ordered some supper, and Dick got impatient and went to find the food. He went into the kitchen, and the woman who was doing the cooking screamed at him to get out of there. He slipped on the greasy floor and gashed his head. The wound looked bad enough to need stitches, but when we got Dick to the hospital he was fighting mad. He wouldn't let the doctor do the stitching, and we had to get orderlies to hold him down. It left him with a big scar, and today he still doesn't know how he got it. He's convinced we got into an argument and I beat the crap out of him. He would go around town asking guys if they knew how he'd got to finish up in hospital with sixteen stitches.

The rest of that summer was much more satisfactory. We bought a small speedboat with an 85-horsepower engine, and each day we'd drive up to Lake Diefenbaker to water-ski. The days followed each other in exactly the same routine. We'd arrive at the lake around 7:00 A.M., water-ski until noon hour, when our arms were about ready to fall off, and then we'd cook up hamburgers. We would spend the afternoon lazing around the lake, catching a little sun, winding down, and then at around five o'clock we'd resume the water-skiing until dusk. Brenda, who was smart, had finished school that January, and I had thirty thousand bucks. So we had the summer to ourselves. I remember turning to her one afternoon and saying, "Brenda, no one ever had it better, did they?" It seemed that nothing existed beyond this beautiful girl and the lake, which was so quiet until the little engine snarled into life, and you didn't want this summer to end, because it was so perfect.

Everything before me was so exciting. I was in control of my future. The NHL had acknowledged me, my dedication through all the levels of minor hockey. And I felt that I had made all the right moves. I was very fortunate to get myself a wife like Brenda. I hadn't made any conscious decision that a hockey player needed a certain kind of girl to stand up to all the pressures of the business, but I did know, right away, that Brenda would be able to handle those pressures. For me it was the luckiest of accidents, because I would have married her anyway.

When we'd discussed marriage, I called Herb Pinder and asked what he thought the pros would think of a kid my age being married. Pinder said that it might concern some club officials, but then the biggest problem with young players is that they get caught in the bright lights and have difficulty settling down to the job at hand. It might be that the idea of having someone who knew where he was going and what he had to do would be appealing at draft time. A guy with a wife and maybe a young baby would have a clearer idea of his responsibilities and his priorities. I said that was exactly the way I'd figured it.

I had also been careful not to suggest that I wanted a bidding war between Toronto and Cincinnati. That kind of business might win you a few more bucks up front, but in the long run I believe it is probably counterproductive. It is better to let a general manager know that you have some standards, that you have some idea of morality. It is also good not to have him disgusted with you before you actually lace up your skates.

I wanted to prove that I was prepared to be the best professional a hockey club ever hired, and that was the reason I cut short our summer on the lake to go to skating school. Toronto had suggested that they would like all their draft choices to attend the skating lessons at the hockey school in Huron Park, Ontario. Jack Valiquette, who had been drafted in the first round, decided not to attend. I really couldn't believe it.

As I saw it, you got one chance to make it big in hockey, one kick at the can, and you were a fool if you didn't go for it with everything you had. You had to take advantage of every opportunity. You never knew what you might need down the road, some little skill, some insight. What was giving up ten days of summer, even that summer we were having beside Lake Diefenbaker? We weren't ordered to go to Huron Park, but I told Brenda that it would be foolish not to volunteer.

Bill Mahoney, who is now coach of the Minnesota North Stars, ran the course, and he did a tremendous job. He had so much to tell somebody like me. The coaches analysed a player's stride and then worked on getting maximum effect. They spent a lot of time on improving our ability to make an explosive start. Most of the guys on the course — a couple I remember particularly were Nick Fotiu and John Wensink — were like me. They realized they had limitations, and they wanted to do all they could to improve. We had a practice each day and then scrimmages each night. Everybody worked hard because there was so much to learn, and you felt you were drawing some benefit from every session.

I would lie on my cot each night and say to myself, "How the hell can Jack Valiquette turn his back on something like this? Who the hell does he think he is?" He was a first-round choice, and I guess he thought he had it made. What he didn't realize was how quickly it could all be unmade. To be honest, neither did I.

8

Tiger Williams would learn quickly enough that professional sport can spring a trapdoor on even the most committed and combative of its performers, but when his fall came, so swiftly and so shockingly, he would have one comfort. He would at least be spared any agony of remorse. No one had prepared more thoroughly than Williams for his first NHL training camp. He ran, he bicycled, he played tennis and he lifted weights. He saw his body as a machine, but it was also like a tabernacle — battered and calloused by the years in Peewee and Bantam, Midget and Junior — but a tabernacle nevertheless. Such reverence for the body of an athlete had been encouraged by the coaches, Murray and McMillan and Dunn, and by his father. And on the journey to Toronto, a meandering trip through North Dakota and Wisconsin and the Great Lakes country, it was dramatically reinforced by Torchy Schell.

Schell was a former RCMP officer in Regina whose ability to detect the difference between a flashy Junior hockey player and one who had the qualities necessary for survival in the NHL had made him a highly respected Western scout for the Toronto Maple Leafs. Schell had recognised these qualities in Williams long before his final year in Junior, and the reports to Toronto had been remarkable for their lack of caution. When a scout recommends a Junior player, he is putting his reputation on the line. The cost of drafting, the investment of time and expertise, becomes a rebuke to the scout if his player reveals major flaws in temperament or moral fibre or simple ability. But the reports that landed on the desk of Jim Gregory and King Clancy spoke of tremendous spirit, a thirst for success and an absolute ruthlessness about the business of winning. Toronto Maple Leafs just couldn't go wrong with Tiger Williams, Schell declared. And then, having made the declaration, he wanted to do everything he could to protect his professional investment.

He persuaded Williams that rather than fly to Toronto for training camp, he should travel by road. Schell would drive, and as he did he could pass on some tips, help the player to prepare mentally for the great trial of training camp, the place where professional hockey players were forged — and imposters were flushed out, like rabbits in the prairie stubble. It was an odyssey of unlimited optimism for Williams. For Schell, the challenge was to implant some sense that in professional hockey, as in so many other areas of life, nothing could be taken for granted. There were so many pitfalls, so many ways to make killing mistakes. Indeed, on the first leg of the journey, Schell got a chance to make an important point. It had to do with the way a professional should treat customs officials.

When we stopped at the Saskatchewan-North Dakota line, I got out of the car to stretch my legs and breathe the air. It was a beautiful morning and, of course, I felt good. I was about to conquer the world. I noticed a dead sparrow lying on top of a garbage can, and just then the U.S. border guard came to the car. I pointed to the sparrow and said, "I see you haven't had your breakfast yet."

I might just as well have insulted Old Glory. The guy went crazy. He went through the trunk, had all our baggage out. He even squirted out some of Torchy's shaving cream. We were stuck at that little crossing for more than an hour. Torchy said that he hoped I had learned a lesson. An NHL player crosses the border so many times during a season that the best idea was to go about your business, go quietly. I was a professional now, and I had to act accordingly. He went on in that vein for the best part of sixteen hundred miles.

Before our night stops at the motels, Torchy would put me out of the car five or six miles from our destination, and I would run in, shower, and then go to dinner. We ate well.

Torchy had a good appetite, and we lived high at the expense of the Maple Leafs. It was wonderful after all the truck stops of the Juniors. Over the steaks, Torchy would talk about the pressures of training camp and what I might expect. He said it would be harder than I could imagine but he had every confidence in me. I said to him, "Torchy, there's nothing to worry about. I'm going to be fine." I was convinced. I wasn't whistling in the dark. So when it happened, I was stunned.

What happened was that I suddenly realized I wasn't as good as I'd always thought. Nobody had ever told me I couldn't skate. But in training camp guys were flying by me. I couldn't keep up. It was the scariest feeling I've ever had. There was an additional problem, which was magnified because I was a rookie. On my first day at training camp, I had tied my laces much too tight, and they had cut into me like razor blades. I was in a terrible mess after that first session, and I spent the rest of training camp trying to repair the damage. I should have told the trainers, but I was scared that someone might think I was whining. I was so desperate to make a good impression.

At the back of my mind I had this constant thought, "Holy shit, these guys are committed to paying me nearly half a million dollars." I got very tense, and before every practice or scrimmage I tried to do something to improve my ankle wounds. I'd spray on something called "tough skin," dab it with baby powder, put on some more tough skin and wrap on bandages. The result was that I never felt really relaxed and comfortable for the entire training camp. I kept telling myself that I was getting paid about a hundred dollars an hour and I just had to crank it up.

And, of course, I had a reputation to protect. I was the cocky kid from the West who was going to put some fight into this great old club that had become soft-centred. I was very cocky with the media and very aggressive on the ice — and inside I was screaming. Things were going on that were beyond my control. For the first time in my life, I was in a situation I wasn't really sure about. So I made some noise, made statements about how tough I was — and pushed myself into a corner. I had to deliver. On my first shift in a training camp scrimmage, I started pounding on Ian Turnbull, who was the club's first-round draft choice from the previous year. I had two more

Tiger Williams' father, Taffy, and two sons,
Morgan (left) and Tiger (right).

Williams' first rink — The Souris River.

Weyburn's main street in the 1950s.

Leonard, Ann and David in 1956.

Tiger at age fourteen.

Tiger (third from left, front row) with his
Peewee team, the Weyburn Maple Leafs.

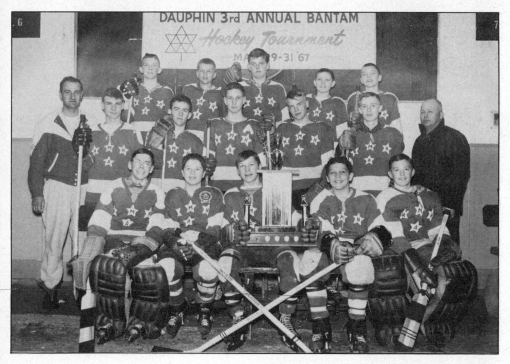

Bantam days. Williams (second from right, first row) with the Weyburn Beavers.

Williams ready for Junior action with
the Swift Current Broncos.

A family portrait: wife Brenda stands beside
Tiger, who is holding daughter Clancy.
Son Ben is seated in front.

Gerry Dean, trainer, David Harris, club doctor,
Kenny Flager and Tiger gather around the
Clarence Campbell Trophy. (Bill Cunningham)

Williams shows authority on the boards for the
Toronto Maple Leafs. (Barry Gray *The Toronto
Sun*)

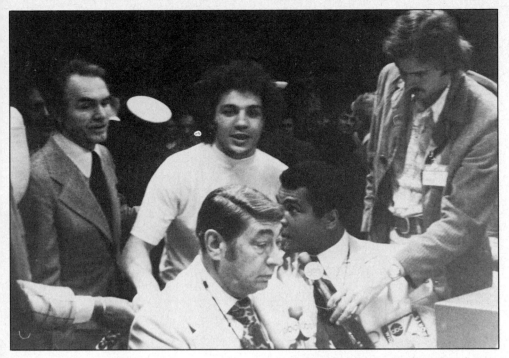

Tiger Williams (standing, centre) joins
other big names: Howard Cosell (seated,
centre) and Muhammed Ali.

Williams on the road with the Toronto Maple
Leafs. (Mike Peak, *The Toronto Sun*)

Hold on, Tiger. Linesman John D'Amico restrains Williams.
(Barry Gray, *The Toronto Sun*)

Eyes on the puck! Williams
concentrates on the job for the
Leafs. (Robert Shaver)

Williams and Bob Kelly from the Philadelphia
team are restrained by officials, but not for
long. (Ed Moran, *The Toronto Sun*)

Putting pressure on the North Stars, Williams
performs typically in front of the net.
(Frank Lennon, *The Toronto Star*)

Williams greets Prime Minister Trudeau.
(Dick Farrell, *The Toronto Sun*)

Tiger and son Ben. (Frank Lennon, *The Toronto Star*)

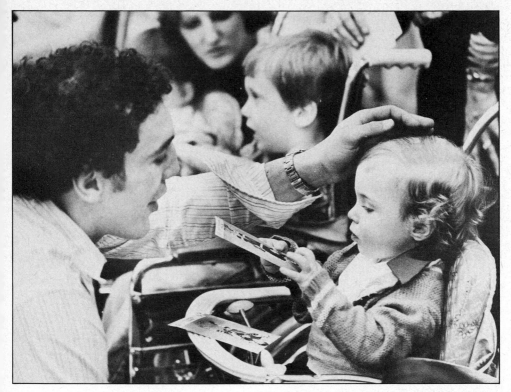

Tiger and friend. Williams' special interest in
the handicapped started in his first years in
Toronto. (Bob Olsen)

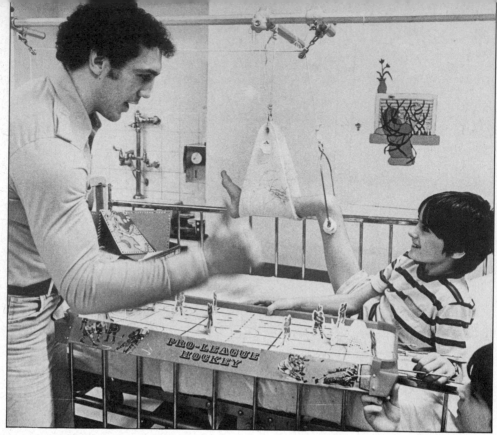

Tiger visiting a fan in hospital.
(Ron Bull, *The Toronto Star*)

Lanny McDonald, left, and Williams put on
their own hospital playoffs.
(Ron Bull, *The Toronto Star*)

fights in that first scrimmage. The trouble was that the fighting, like the skating, wasn't going too well.

It was as though the tension had taken away all my mind control. I was deeply troubled by the way so many guys were outskating me, and when we got to the exhibiton games, I was just running at guys indiscriminately. I'd run at everybody on my first shift, and I'd fall down six times. Whatever I did, it seemed to turn bad. I couldn't do anything with the puck, and the odd goal I scored was nothing: a scuffle in front of the net, a deflection, maybe a jam-in. But I was supposed to be both a fighter and a scorer, and every night I went to my bed a little stunned. But mostly I felt sick with worry. I called my dad and said, "Jeez, there are guys here who are drinking a skinful of beer, and they're still going past me on the ice. Dad, I don't really know what's happening to me." One day I had been ready to conquer the world, the next I was like some kid going to a new school for the first time. I recall thinking, "Tiger, you're marooned in whale shit."

It was Keith Magnuson of the Chicago Black Hawks who condemned me to the minors. I'd been getting plenty of ice time in the exhibition games, but I hadn't been able to use it to advantage. The more I tried, the worse it got. Against the Black Hawks, Magnuson caught me completely by surprise. He was just leaving the Chicago bench as I skated off the ice. He let me have it. It was a complete sucker punch. He put my lights out. I couldn't see a damned thing. The linesman led me to the box. When my penalty was up, I just kept banging the glass of the box, because everything was still a blur, and I needed someone to collect me and guide me back to our bench. I felt terrible back in the dressing room.

Eventually my vision cleared, but there was no relief from the reality of what was happening to me. I was getting my ass kicked out of the National Hockey League before the start of my first season. It was so hard to take! I had made so many promises, to my father, to Brenda, to King Clancy and Harold Ballard. I had been living my life for this chance to play in the big league, and now I felt empty and confused and, for the first time in my life, truly beaten. Of course, I had taken many hammerings, but no one had ever been able to persuade me that they could get the better of me. I might lose a battle or two but, as sure as hell, I was going to win the war.

81

Two days after Magnuson made me look so bad, I was sent down to the minors. A while ago in Chicago, I had thought of Phoenix with disdain, rejected it as being too far from the real heartbeats of hockey. Now I was being sent to Oklahoma. Nobody took me to dinner to discuss it. I was given a plane ticket and told to go. Herb Pinder spoke with Jim Gregory, who said, "He not only can't skate, he can't fight." Gregory's words burned through me all the way to Oklahoma. I felt battered, but I did say, "Well, they can send me down, but they can't keep me down."

In one sense it was good for me to go down. It underlined the challenge facing a guy of my limited natural ability. It told me how much physical conditioning I needed if I was going to make it as a fighter and a player. When I came out of Swift Current, I had a notion that I would have to work hard, but I didn't know anything about the science of looking after your body. I didn't know that when your legs were really aching after practice, you had lactic acid. I didn't know about VO_2, volume oxygen, about the value of building your aerobic system on a year-long routine. But at that first NHL training camp, a lot of things became very clear to me.

You could go a long way on will and heart and the power of ambition but you couldn't go all the way. You needed something extra. You needed to be mentally sharp, and your physical conditioning had to be perfect. For me the need for deep stamina was vital because of the fighting. I had to be able to fight long and hard and still be a factor in the play. Already I had seen how quickly the pace and the action of the NHL could drain you.

All this was going through my mind on the flight to Oklahoma. There were a lot of stops on the way, and I had plenty of time to think about the shock of that training camp. There had been the shock of realizing how much I had to do, the shock of seeing players I'd admired for so long abusing their bodies with booze. I knew now that it wasn't all as simple as it had seemed back in Swift Current and up on the lake water-skiing away those hot days beneath the prairie sky. In Oklahoma, Brenda and I found an apartment near the rink. It was in a smart new building with a swimming pool. I told Brenda not to settle down. We would be back in Toronto soon enough.

But first there was more humiliation. In my first game for the Oklahoma City Blazers, a season opener against Omaha, in the first minute I got into a big fight with Ken Houston. I thought that would set the pattern for my time down there. But a few games later, I completely failed to rise to a challenge presented by my old rival Bob Gassoff, who was then with Denver. He had parked himself in front of our bench, challenged the whole bunch of us, and I just didn't react. I'd always said, "However tough you're going to play, I'm going to play tougher," but on this occasion, I didn't see the point of taking on Gassoff. I said, "Oh shit, I've been fighting Bob Gassoff all my life. What does this mean?" And Gassoff, the crazy bastard, just skated away. My behaviour didn't go down too well with the rest of the guys.

They were thinking, "Here's this hotshot kid with the tough reputation who's getting the big bucks, and he lets this guy Bob Gassoff thumb his nose at the whole team." One of the players, a guy called Mike Sauter, came over to me and said, "Don't let that happen again; someone comes over to this bench, you get the hell out of here and whomp the bastard. I don't care if he's eight feet tall, that's your goddamned job."

I took the advice to heart, and I just thrashed and battered my way through the first half of that season. I felt better when I looked around the minor league and saw a lot of good guys down there, like Guy Chouinard in Omaha and Bob Bourne in Fort Worth. Every team had three or four regulars who would make it to the NHL. But there were also a lot of discontented players down there in the minors, and so a lot of things could become causes of friction. Two things were important in my case. First, Jack Valiquette and I were probably making nearly as much as the rest of the Oklahoma team put together, and some people were bound to resent that. And second, probably most important, I refused to join in the dressing room routine.

The schedule for a lot of guys was to go to morning practice, then slide off to a bar until four or five o'clock before going home for some supper and a long sleep. I told the guys that there was too much drinking and that I didn't want any part of it. It didn't make me popular, and Pat Boutette in particular began to needle me. One day in the dressing room, I turned on him, told him he was a mouthy little bastard and he'd better get off my case. I said I didn't care what anyone wanted to do with their bodies and their careers. I knew where I was going. I was going back to the big time. I'd made a couple of mistakes, missed a chance or two, but I hadn't failed because of any lack of effort or thought.

Maybe it had all gotten out of perspective when I first went to Toronto. I'd forgotten how to relax, I hadn't prepared myself as well as I'd thought. But there would be no mistake next time. When most of the other guys were drinking beer and listening to country music, I was working out those hot afternoons. When I couldn't skate, I ran. And in the games — which were generally watched by about two thousand fans, with four thousand or so turning up on a beer night — I was gaining confidence. I had a lot of fights and I won most of them. The goals were coming, too. I was seeing the relationship between work and confidence on the ice.

In certain situations, a fight can relax you and still get the adrenalin up to exactly the right pitch. But you have to be able to take the punishment and stay strong. A lot of guys are physically and mentally wasted by a fight. In the NHL later, I saw Jack Valiquette absolutely drained by a fight in Pittsburgh, and Ian Turnbull was once unable to finish a game because he put too much into a bout. But it seemed to me that I was gaining strength and momentum with every fight. By Christmas, I had scored 16 goals and I was ready. I was leading the league with Eugene Sobchuk — Dennis's older brother — and my ear was close to the ground. I was listening for the word from Toronto.

The way things were going up in Toronto made it inevitable that the word would come. The Maple Leafs still had that soft centre, the one I had been brought up to fill last fall. The position of the club was getting more serious with every game. Morale hit zero when Eddie Shack took a bad beating from Bob Gassoff and the rest of the guys just let it happen. There was also a bad situation when no one reacted to the spearing of Rod Seiling by Bobby Clarke. The Leafs, who not so long ago had been Stanley Cup winners and giants across the land, had become a club who could be easily pushed around, and the fact that it was being publicly announced each game was driving King Clancy crazy. When Shack took his beating, Clancy apparently turned to Jim Gregory and said, "That's enough. Bring up the kid."

I got the call on New Year's Day. My bags had always been half-packed, and as Brenda drove me to the airport, I told her, "This is it. We're saying good-bye to Oklahoma City." I had five stops on the twelve-hour journey to New York City, and then there was a taxi ride out to Long Island, where the Leafs were playing the Islanders the following night. I had plenty of time to assess the changes that had come to me in those forty games in the minors. I saw more clearly than ever that to make a life of being a pro I had to keep to a very straight line, both physically and mentally. Some guys could take a chance or two. Maybe Jack Valiquette had enough talent to get by without killing himself in practice, without pushing himself to the limit of his physical resources. But I knew now that it was impossible for me. I had to slog it every step of the way.

Driving up to Toronto with Torchy Schell had been a kind of fantasy. Now, as the taxi rolled along the Long Island Expressway, I had no illusions at all. Basically, I was alone, and it would always be that way until my life as a hockey player was over. Of course I would have to have some allies. In the end, survival may be based on the strength of your own will, but it helps if you have some friends. So I was pleased when I got to the Long Island Inn that the first two guys to say hello and wish me good luck were Lanny McDonald and Darryl Sittler.

I knew McDonald from his days in Medicine Hat, and I admired him a lot. Sittler was a class player and a good man. Over the next few years, he would show me exactly how good a man he was; he always showed character on and off the ice, sometimes under the heaviest of pressure. Sometimes you can make snap decisions about guys and be pretty sure you've got a true handle on them, and that was the way it was with Sittler. You didn't need much insight to see that he was a genuine player and a genuine guy. After the trouble in Oklahoma, the feeling that so many guys were not serious about their careers and resented people who were, it was a relief to be accepted by people of this quality.

But I guess there is some self-interest in all of us. They were in the early stages of their careers. They were good players worried that their club was not shaping up as a winner, and maybe they thought that the kid from the prairie could do a job, help himself and help everybody. That's the way I saw it, too, and McDonald was very strong in his support. We were to be very close for four years, and then we would find ourselves in a position to take money out of each other's pockets, and there is no point in denying that we're not as close now as we used to be. It's sad, but so are many of the realities of life. Back then, everything was simple. I needed those guys, and I guess they figured they needed me — or some other crazy kid who would make the right moves and get something stirring in the dressing room.

I didn't get too much ice time in that first game on the Island, and Frank Orr, a hockey writer for the *Toronto Star*, offered the opinion that I wouldn't last ten games. I got into a fight with Garry Howatt, a former Flin Flon scrapper, and took a penalty in the first period. I didn't do much in the game, but it was wonderful just being there, getting the feel of the big league. Gary Sabourin was right wing and Sittler centre on my line. It was really just a question of feeling my way, trying to make it clear that I meant business this time. I got just four shifts, but it did give me the opportunity to start a feud with Howatt, who was one of only three or four guys in the league who was around my size and still willing to drop the gloves and really fight. I had a sneaking regard for the scrappy little bastard.

From Long Island we went to St Louis, which had a tough team then, and right off the face-off Barclay Plager hit me with an extremely hard shot to the face, and I automatically dropped my gloves and wheeled on him. It was a good fight, and a photograph of it went right across the country. It was the kind of publicity and impact I needed; but I was worried by the extent of the job, worried that I might get swept away by the overall weaknesses of this club's temperament. We made a swing over to the West Coast with games in Los Angeles, Oakland and Vancouver, and in L.A. I was in the middle of another crisis. The Kings beat us 8–0 and the only good thing about the game from my point of view was that I got so much ice time after it was clear we were well beaten. I was playing everywhere — I even had one shift on defence — and I was hitting everybody.

It seemed to me that a lot of guys were just plain scared: scared of the fighting, scared of making mistakes and looking bad. And maybe that was the explanation for all the drinking. Or perhaps it was the cause of it. I was bitter about the way gifted players were spending so much time in the bars and the edge of my bitterness was that their drinking was probably hurting the team and threatening my future. I had been brought up from Oklahoma to inject some life into the team, and here we were being dismantled by Los Angeles.

I had so much tension on this trip that I couldn't sleep. I had to throw away the bed sheets because they were so wet with sweat. I would get up in the middle of the night and take a cold shower to try to cool down. At best, I was getting two or three hours of sleep, and I'd always wake up shaking and sweating. I had my problems, and the way the guys were drinking was beginning to prey on my mind. I felt it was shocking that a kid in his first few games in the NHL was sick with tension and worry while so many guys who had so much more talent and experience seemed to be saying, "Oh, what the hell, have another drink." It seemed to me that they were cheating themselves and the people who paid their wages. And they might just be cheating me out of a career.

On the morning flight up to Oakland Jim McKenny was sitting with Blaine Stoughton. McKenny had a 26-ounce bottle of liquor and they kept asking the stewardess for coke. After they'd had about half a dozen cokes each, one stewardess asked to smell their drinks, and there was an incident between McKenny and the girl. He grabbed her and made an obscene remark, and she got very upset. I was very upset, too. What I was upset about was the fact that McKenny wouldn't be able to play that night. He was abusing his body, and everybody on the team would suffer.

When we got to Vancouver, my frustrations, and maybe my tension, came to the surface. I went to Sittler and McDonald and said that I was concerned about the level of drinking among some of our teammates. Red Kelly had said that there would be an 11 o'clock curfew that night (we played at five o'clock the following day) and he expected us to stick to it. I felt a lot of responsibility because Ferguson was my roommate, and he was one of the guys who liked to take a drink on the road. I told him that I expected him to be in the room by 11:00 P.M., and if he wasn't he would be locked out. We were staying at the Hotel Vancouver, and some of the guys had strolled over to the nearby Ritz Hotel for lunch. I'd gone over, too, but I left after lunch. I was concerned because some of the guys were getting into the beer, and it seemed to me that it was a hell of a long time to curfew.

Around seven o'clock, I went back to the Ritz to check out Ferguson, and I reminded him about curfew. I guess it was George's bad luck that I was his roommate. Throughout my career, I've never been a popular roommate. I've always tried to keep the guys in line. A few of the players had been drinking from early afternoon, and I sensed they were picking up on my conversation with Ferguson, but I didn't give a damn what they thought, because I was preparing for my fifth NHL game and I'd been told by Red Kelly that I had ten games to make it in the league.

Ferguson came into our room about 10:45 P.M. He was in bad shape, stumbling around. Then the phone rang for him. He spoke for a moment, then hung up and said he was going out again. I said there was no way he was going out. I took his boots and hid them. He was swearing and blustering, and I just pushed him down on the bed and said that if he didn't stop, I would hit him, really hit him. By this time a kid could have handled him. There was a lot of noise and some of the other players came to the room to see what was going on. Quite a number of the guys were hostile towards me, while Normie Ullman, Sabourin, Sittler and McDonald clearly agreed with my attitude. Ferguson went off to Dunc Wilson's room, and then somebody put in a call to Red Kelly. Before Kelly appeared, Ferguson came out of Wilson's room holding his hand. It was broken.

When the story reached the press, it had Ferguson breaking his hand on the jaw of the kid from Saskatchewan, which I thought was strange, because, the condition he was in, he hardly laid a glove on me. A few weeks later, I was told that Ferguson had been so angry and frustrated when he got into Wilson's room, he just started to flail around and finally smashed his hand into the wall. When we got back to Toronto, I was swamped by the press. Everyone wanted to know the inside story. The final public version was that Ferguson and I had had a disagreement, that we were incompatible and the tensions of a difficult road trip had got to us. There was all that kind of bullshit flying around.

What I had done, in fact, was touch on something that was being felt increasingly by the players who formed the core of the team. Sittler and McDonald supported me strongly against those guys who thought I was pushing myself into the situation. After the incident, Dave Keon, the team captain, called a meeting between the players and Kelly, and the general feeling was that discipline had to be tightened. What could I say to the press? I couldn't tell them that six of our players openly boozed it up on the road. That wasn't my job or my realm. All I had done was react as honestly as I could to a situation I found bewildering. It was a tough situation for me, because I didn't have too long to prove myself, and I certainly didn't want to make enemies. I was desperate to make the club, and under those circumstances, you need all the friends you can find.

At least I had stood by my principles. I didn't have any sympathy for a guy who cheated himself, his teammates and his club, and there was a lot of that going on. It was very disillusioning. There was even some disillusionment on one of the biggest nights of my life. Normie Ullman and his wife, Bibs, invited Brenda and me out to a restaurant and bar with some of the other guys and their wives. It was the first time a big-name player, a guy whose face you might find on one of my old hockey cards, had invited me out, and I was very flattered. But there was also a sadness to the evening. Eddie Shack was in the company, and with him was Dick Duff, another player I'd admired so much. Duff was so drunk he couldn't really handle himself, and I learned later that Shack had taken him in and was trying to help him through a tough time. It was another example to me of how the pressures of the game could affect people. Shack's help and Duff's own decision to go to Alcoholics Anonymous saved that situation, but at the time I thought, "Hey, all those guys who once seemed to walk on water are all falling in front of me!" It made me both mad and confused.

Up to then I had always been so sure of everything. Now it was hard to make sense of a lot of situations. Things were going on around me that weren't always what they seemed. A good example of this was an incident with Bill "Cowboy" Flett. It happened before practice at the Gardens one morning. I was always first on the ice, and I was surprised on this occasion when Flett came out with me. Usually, he'd only beat Red Kelly on to the ice by about ten seconds. Flett started horsing around, and we dropped our sticks and gloves and wrestled.

89

Suddenly, Flett rolled on the ice and screamed "Get the trainer." He was helped off the ice by the trainer and taken to hospital. He had stretched ligaments; he would be out for six weeks. Naturally, I felt terrible.

Jim Gregory called me up to his office and really laid into me. He said that if I was going to fool around, I could go back to where I came from. The NHL was no place for people who didn't take the job seriously — which in the circumstances was a laughable statement.

At the end of the season, I was having a beer with Sittler, when he said, "Do you know what really happened with Cowboy?" I said no, other than the fact the whole business still made me feel lower than a whale's belly, even though deep down I still felt I hadn't really touched him. Sittler told me that Flett had come to that practice injured. He had hurt himself skidooing the night before and realized that if the club knew how he had wrecked his knee, he might not get paid. "Cowboy knew you would be on the ice early," said Sittler. Flett had set me up.

I didn't make anything of it, but it was the kind of thing that worked on a kid's confidence, made you wonder about all your ideas of what the game meant and then the reality of it. I still had the idea that being part of a team was the greatest thing. I had always played the game to better myself, but not at the expense of other guys. I felt you got out of the game exactly what you put in, and it kept surprising me that so many people were prepared to take short-cuts, and, at the same time, do whatever was necessary to protect themselves, even to the point of framing a teammate.

There wasn't much relief at all for me that first year. Keon, the great player, the captain of the Leafs, did me no favours. In fact, he wore me down with his criticisms. He never did what I thought a captain should. He never took the new kid to one side and tried to help him. He never encouraged, never said, "Hey, that was a hell of a check you threw," or, "Good game." No, he only had criticisms. He would say, "What the hell are doing out there?" or "You couldn't pass the puck if your life depended on it, you son of a bitch." It didn't seem to occur to him that a young player needed the odd positive comment. Plenty of people had kicked my ass, but no one had ever nagged away at me like Keon. It went on for so long, I finally snapped. We were together in an elevator in St. Louis. He was making his usual remarks, digging into me, and I grabbed his tie and said, "Look, Keon, I don't need this shit, get off my back or I'll break your neck." He left me alone after that.

Harold Ballard was different. He could be critical, could come into the dressing room raging mad after a bad loss. But I knew how to deal with Ballard. Guy Kinnear, who was then equipment manager of the Leafs and skipper of Ballard's yacht in the summer, gave me the tip. He said, "If Mr. Ballard gets on your case, just stand up to him, show you're not afraid." At the time I thought Kinnear was setting me up, but I found out later that he had spoken the truth. What happened was that Ballard caught me in a bad mood after a game, and when he said, "You goddamned little stubble-jumper from Saskatchewan," I replied, "It's better than being a fat bastard from Ontario." After that, Ballard and I got along fine. If you put your tail between your legs, Ballard would be disgusted. You had to show him you had balls. If you didn't, he would drive you away from Toronto and maybe even the league. He did that to Inge Hammarstrom.

I promised him the hide from the first bear I killed, and he was delighted when I took it down to Maple Leaf Gardens. He put it in his office. Unfortunately my first bear was a bit of a midget, and I was tempted to wait for a bigger animal. But I'd said he would get the first one, and I kept my word.

In some ways, Ballard and I were the same. We hated to lose, and we didn't care what people thought about us as long as we won. He would pay out big money for success, be so desperate to be seen as a winner. And with me it was a question of not letting a night go by without asking myself, "Did I do enough today? Could I have done any more to get on in this goddamned business?" Ballard saw this in me. And he was smart enough to detect the difference between those players who made a show about losing and those who were really hurt by it. Ballard could tell that when we lost I would hurt. I wouldn't often make a lot of noise, throw stuff around the dressing room. Everybody did that routine in Junior but I tried to grow out of that. All that stuff is really bullshit. When you've lost, it's no time to be making a lot of noise. You should sit down and think about what you did, and, more important, what you didn't do. Sometimes you find that the guys who carry on most

91

about a loss did the least to prevent it. Sometimes you feel like saying, "Hey, pal, who do you think you're kidding?"

In time, Ballard came to look after me quite a bit. Once he heard I was doing some advertising stunt for a sporting goods firm and he also found out what I was getting paid, which was something around $500. He said that I was being exploited. He called me into his office and asked me what I really needed in the line of hunting and fishing gear. I said that I was looking for a good shotgun. He called up the firm to say there was no way one of his players was going to do a commercial at such a low rate, and if they wanted my services, they would have to give me a couple of good shotguns. I got two beautiful Winchesters worth around $2,000 each. To him it was no big deal, but it was important to me. He was giving me some kind of status, saying "Hey, don't horse around with this kid, he's one of my boys."

When you play for a guy like Ballard, who you know has a sentimental streak but who also detests losers, it is good to get the odd signal of approval. Sometimes he would mix up his signals, but I never got the feeling that he doubted my value. Everyone needs such reassurance from time to time, I guess, and if you don't have it in somewhere like the NHL you can be in deep trouble. The way I played the game, it was important to get some reassurance, and I had the feeling Ballard would always be behind me.

I suppose drink is a reassurance, and maybe some of the players took it during the season because it pushed the pressures to one side for a little while. What they didn't realize was that it complicated everything, when their lives had to be simple, straightforward. They had a few years to make their money, and that should have been the priority; but, for one reason or another, a lot of them slipped into drinking and woke up to find that they needed it for a lot more than an hour or two's relaxation.

In some cases, the anger I felt about the drinking didn't prevent me from liking a guy a lot. McKenny was a good example. I used to call him "tomato-head," because he'd drink all night and then come to practice dehydrated and without food or sleep, and he'd work so hard in practice that his face would turn bright red. But I liked the guy, because he was funny and very kind, and we got on well even though he knew how much

I loathed the boozing. Borje Salming would either not drink a drop or go all the way, really fill his boots. Once, he and McKenny were driving the wrong way down a main drag in Toronto; the cops stopped them and recognized them. When they opened the car doors, McKenny fell into the street. "Have you been drinking?" one of the cops asked. "No," said McKenny, "I always look like this." One day McKenny brought his five-year-old son, Jason, down to the rink, and when Red Kelly saw the boy he came over to say hello. Jason looked up at the coach and said, "My mum thinks you're a frigging idiot." McKenny didn't blink. He said, "Hey, I don't necessarily have the same views as my wife." Yes, he was a funny bastard and he had a lot of ability, but the booze kept tugging at him, and you wonder what he could have done if he had ever got free of it. In fact, when he got away from the pressures of the game, he brought his life more under control, which was good to see.

Slowly I won over the respect of some of those guys who thought I was just some little jerk up from the prairie who wanted to make a big name for himself with the management. Maybe they saw that I was ready to give everything I had for the team and that the Ferguson episode came from my convictions and nothing else. I wasn't playing any angles. I was doing things according to my conscience.

My first NHL goal came after ten games. It was against Montreal in the Forum. It was the winning goal in a 5–3 game. Ronnie Ellis and I were two-on-one, and Ellis was wide on the boards. He gave a nice pass, and as the defenceman came over, I put it right into the roof of the net. It was so sweet seeing it go in. I did my first dance, my first "Tiger Rag" in the NHL.

After the game, I called Bernie Jordan, a guy back in Weyburn who drove a Saskatchewan Power truck and used to drive me crazy talking about the goddamned Canadiens. I asked him how he liked what I had done to his team.

9

Scoring on the Montreal Canadiens and achieving that sublime satisfaction was in the nature of a bonus. That night in the Forum, fantasy had become real life. But several days before, in the office of Maple Leaf general manager Jim Gregory, the most important victory of Williams's career had been confirmed. Gregory told him to bring his wife up from Oklahoma and arrange some accommodation in Toronto. The kid had made his point and paid his dues. He might not be a great skater or fluent stickhandler, but he had something that this rich club had lacked for too long. He had intensity of purpose that transcended the normal commitments of a professional, so much that coach Red Kelly sometimes worried about his welfare.

His willingness to fight, both on and off the ice, had become a fact of life with the club. When the gifted Toronto defenceman Ian Turnbull had an angry dispute with Red Kelly in the dressing room between periods of a tense game, Williams placed himself between the men and said to Turnbull, "You touch him and I'll kill you." At the end-of-season party held for the players at the Toronto nightspot Jervis House, Williams thought one of the bouncers was behaving with excessive zeal, and he took it upon himself to make the point. A fight followed, and a teammate managed to get Williams out of the club before the police arrived. Ironically, the teammate was Ian Turnbull, who had been fighting at

Williams's side after the other bouncers joined the fray. The following day Williams was again called to the office of Jim Gregory. This time, the general manager told him to get out of town, handing him a cheque for his bonus money. The club wanted Williams to lie low for a while.

But it was clear enough that he would be welcomed back in the fall. Williams was so sure about this that he made arrangements to buy a house in Mississauga. The Williamses spent some time dallying in Florida and then returned to Saskatchewan for the summer. That summer brought more good news: Brenda was pregnant with their first child. The hockey player was twenty-one years old. He had had a full year. From now on, professionally at least, he would be travelling in the fast lane.

I got a hell of a charge out of being a Maple Leaf. Every day there was a little reminder that you were a somebody. I didn't want to get carried away with it, lose any sense of who I was and what I had to do, but I'd be lying if I didn't admit that it was very important for me to be recognized.

Once, my brother Leonard and I went into a furniture store in the Italian-Portuguese quarter of Toronto. Within minutes the place was full of hockey fans. They were even milling around in the street. I said to Leonard, "You slip out, get the car and drive a couple of blocks. I'll go out through the back and join you in the car." I signed quite a few autographs, but it would have taken me hours to deal with all those people, and that day I had things to do. As we drove away, Leonard was wide-eyed, and he said, "Holy shit, do you get much of that?" He was excited by it, and he wondered why I hadn't stayed in the store. I said that if you stopped for everybody, you'd never get through a day. But the truth was that I was excited too.

I also knew the importance of the fans. Hockey fans are like the rest of society; a few are outstanding, and the rest are good, bad and, in some cases, outright dingbats. There was that guy who climbed into the penalty box in Los Angeles and tried to attack me. We found out later that he was a professional agitator of athletes; his idea was to provoke a guy, get hit and then sue. The club had to pay him $10,000 after I gave him a few shots. I thought it was outrageous, but it saved money in the long run.

When I play hockey, I have a picture of the fan. He has had a tough day at the office, or the mill or factory, where I could

95

quite easily have had to spend my working life. He may have been wheeling cement at some construction site. Maybe his back is aching. Maybe he's worried about paying some bills, worried about his wife or his kids. And he goes to the rink to be entertained, to be taken away from all these everyday things that bug him. I don't make a god out of the fan, because when it comes to the game, the reality of it, he can't know about some of the things that go into winning a hockey game. Some fans are impressed by obvious things, by the way a guy looks good stickhandling or skating, and this is reasonable, because he has come to the rink to be entertained. But he also wants his team to win, and this is where it gets a little bit complicated. A lot of guys who skate wonderfully and handle the stick as if by magic have no stomach for winning, for battling when things get tough.

The fan idolizes a Gretzky and a Lafleur for good reasons. These are guys of genius. You wonder at their skills, where they get all their natural ability. They are something to see. Below that level, there are many categories of hockey player. I knew I would never be idolized. I didn't have the stuff it required. But I knew I could impress the fans in other ways. I knew I could convince them I was doing all I could on their behalf. No fan could say, "That Williams is stealing the money they pay him." This was important because — and as a player you have to remember the fact — all the money in hockey comes from the fan, whether it is sponsorship money or television money or money that comes straight from the gate. You have to remember this when somebody starts to give you a hard time outside the rink or in a restaurant or a bar. You have to remember that the fans pay the shot. But there is a limit.

An asshole is an asshole whether he's a nuclear physicist or a hockey fan, and sometimes there is a big temptation to drive him one straight between the eyes. You have to resist it, of course. You have to think that for a number of years you are caught up in something that has its own rules, some of which may be very bizarre. But then, there are compensations.

Playing hockey in Toronto, you were made to feel like a big shot. You got to sit in the office of Irving and Karl Ungerman's chicken factory, where influential people gathered, guys who had millions of dollars. You'd be introduced to such people as Toronto mayor David Crombie and Ontario premier William

96

Davis, and you thought to yourself, "Wow, they meet me on equal terms." I was a twenty-one-year-old stubble-jumper from Saskatchewan, but everyone knew my face, knew my name. You saw then the power of professional sports. Hockey seemed as big as anything you could name.

Everyone wanted to know about hockey players, where they lived, what they did in their spare time. The Toronto news media became a part of my life that I was very conscious of. I tried to make their job a little easier, and I reckoned it would help me in the long run. They'd always get a quote from me, something that might spice up a piece on a dull day, or a Hockey Night in Canada interview. During a playoff series with Pittsburgh, Brian McFarlane asked me who I thought was going to win the game, and I told him, "They're done like dinner." People still come up to me and mention that quote, eight years afterwards.

Of course some writers would take advantage, twist the quotes around a bit. Others didn't bother to tidy up the quotes, just slammed them in. And there were times when I was painted as either a full-blown illiterate or a lunatic, and some-times both. But I got on television, and I got a lot of ink. People knew my name, and I realized that that was what it was all about. In some respects I was quite calculating, of course: these writers, some of whom I liked a lot, could help me and my career; and the fans I spent some time with, well, one day they might buy my book.

One thing I didn't calculate was the involvement I had with kids, kids who were really ill and those who were mentally handicapped. Back on the prairie, if a family had a retarded kid, they would hide him; the poor little bastard would be lucky if he got some fresh air. In Toronto we were taken to the Hospital for Sick Children, and at first it used to break me up seeing kids with artificial limbs and third degree burns. I never turned down a request to do something for those kids. And when I went down there, I wouldn't just walk down a few wards with some ding-y nurse. It would irritate the hell out of me when some other guys did that: just whisk through the place, say "Hi," and then piss off in their flashy cars.

I guess you couldn't do a lot, but you could do something. You couldn't give them new limbs or heal their burns, but you could give them something else to think about. You'd talk to them for a while, and you would see their eyes shining, and, Christ, that just had to affect you a little bit. Who the hell were you to have this power to help kids so far behind the eight ball? It's no big deal to want to help kids in that situation. In fact, sometimes you wonder which of you is helping the other most. There are a lot of temptations to think you've got the world by the tail when things are going well, when you're getting the big fat paycheques and everybody wants to say hello. But then you go somewhere like the Hospital for Sick Children, and you realize what a goddamned lottery life is. And if you are ahead of the game, it's useful to be reminded of this from time to time.

The overwhelming feeling I took away from my first year in the NHL, a sense that I'd done well after a shaky start (in the second half of the season I followed the scoring breakthrough in Montreal with nine more goals), but that I had to work harder than most just to survive. That summer of 1975 I couldn't afford to lose all track of time on the waters of Lake Diefenbaker. I went to a skating school in Penticton, B.C., and gave myself the toughest physical program I had ever faced. Laura Stramm ran the school in Penticton, and while it was clear she knew a lot about skating, it was just as obvious that she couldn't be of much help to me. She talked about the theory of skating, the classic moves. This didn't help me at all. It's like when a golfer goes for help with his swing. He wants to make *his* swing work. It's too difficult to re-construct a new, perfectly grooved swing. Laura wanted to change my skating in a way that wasn't possible at that stage of my life. I wanted just to improve the equipment I had. Really, I wanted to make the best of a bad job.

I had heard by the grapevine that the Maple Leafs intended to set new levels of fitness at training camp, and there would be an emphasis on running. There would be a 1½-mile race in which the target time was nine minutes. When I got back to Swift Current, I worked on both speed and fitness. Don Szakacs and Jim Bobick, physical education teachers at the Swift Current high school, would often run with me at seven o'clock in the morning. Often I would run on the Swift Current golf course, and I set myself a circuit of about two miles. Slowly, I moved from one circuit to two, then three and finally four. As I went by groups of golfers, they would shout, "Way to go, Tiger!" and it was a great encouragement. Sometimes I'd say, "I'll pass you bastards again before you reach the sixth green." I had a sense that people were behind me, now that I'd gone up to Toronto and was making a bit of a name for myself. They could see that I was serious about my business.

Some time before training camp, Red Kelly called me to say that there was a Russian guy in Toronto, a Dr. Sasha Mushkin, who had some interesting ideas about skating and balance, and he was running a course. Kelly thought Mushkin could help me. So, of course, I went to Toronto early. Jack Valiquette was also asked to attend, along with Brian Glennie, who was a poor skater. Glennie found the Russian so bizarre that he just walked out. Of the original ten members of the class, only three or four of us saw out the course. I stayed because I thought, well, the coach thinks this joker can help, so what the hell. Dr. Mushkin had some pretty weird ideas, but deep down I thought he was on to something. He had this big black band of elastic stretched across the ice, and we had to charge down the ice and slam into it. It would whip you back like a slingshot. The idea was to always keep your balance, whatever the situation. Dr. Mushkin worked only on situations that took away your balance, and you had to fight to win back some control. He would call us into a circle and go through the guys, saying, "you good boy, you bad boy, you not so good boy, you very dumb boy." He used to say that last phrase to Curt Walker, the big American kid who wasn't too fast on his skates. In fact, the Russian was amazed that any of us was in the NHL, given our skating ability. Mushkin said I was a very good boy, because I worked so hard. Naturally I was the only guy who liked the dumb bastard.

Before we had the big race at training camp, we got this amazing speech from the conditioning coach, Billy Hayward, an ex-drill sergeant of the Canadian Army. He had his hair in a brush cut, and he looked a bit like the sergeant on Gomer Pyle. He said, "The team you play on is called the Maple Leafs, and not only is that the name of your team, it's the flag of your country. You have to be physically and mentally prepared at all times." He was about five feet, eight inches and 240 pounds and looked as solid as a rock. He added, "If any of you want to

99

know what it's like to be physically and mentally prepared, I'll show you."

But then I had a few things to show people, not Hayward, but Kelly and Clancy and Gregory. A year earlier, they had "gonged" me at training camp, and I was determined that this wouldn't happen again. We had the house in Mississauga, and everything was riding on the kind of impression I made over the next few days. I smoked everybody in the big race, running away with it and breaking the nine-minute barrier by nearly fifteen seconds. The only guys in touch with me at all were the Swedes, Salming and Inge Hammarstrom. Winning that race showed my intentions, and I know it raised a few eyebrows. I never wanted to know again that feeling of going down to the minors. I had had it once, and that was enough for a lifetime.

You got the impression that Red Kelly knew he had to produce something that year, that if he didn't make a real run at the Stanley Cup, he could very well be history. He was looking for all the help he could get. It was important for him to have somebody like me, someone ready to run through walls if that was required. He was very considerate to me. Once, I had a bad eye injury, and he was very concerned. He wondered if I should really go out to play. He was a decent man caught in a business that sometimes required a compromise or two. I always told Red that there was no problem: I got good wages and I was prepared to work for them. Red Kelly wasn't the quickest at making decisions on the bench. But if you gave him a little time to resolve a problem, to really think about some aspect of the game, well, he could dazzle you with his brilliance.

Sometimes Kelly would come up with something out of left field — something like pyramid power. He introduced pyramid power as we headed towards a seven-game playoff series with Philadelphia. Red believed that if you had a headache, you could get rid of it by placing a pyramid-shape beneath your pillow. Red believed, and he got us to believe.

We said, "Shit, there must be power in those pyramids. Today you couldn't get the most powerful crane to lift some of those blocks forming the old pyramids in Egypt."

Kelly brought in a guy from the University of Toronto who built four or five special pyramids to put under our bench. I gathered it cost the club about $25,000. The university guy would bring them in and line them up to magnetic north.

Then they brought a bigger pyramid into the dressing room before the third game with Philadelphia. Lanny McDonald sat under the pyramid that night and went out and scored four goals. Before the next game, we were all fighting like hell to sit under the pyramid. Most people agreed that we lost the series because our goaltending wasn't good enough.

Red Kelly got fired at the end of the season. I'm not too sure what happened to the pyramids. I think we burned the bastards.

10

There is a great irony in the life and career of Dave Williams. It is that he is seen clearly as a man of fierce rebellion. He first defies, then mocks authority. He is openly contemptuous of game officials, saving his strongest salvos for the highly experienced referee Bob Myers. Yet in his own mind Williams is a staunch conservative always prepared to give authority the benefit of the doubt.

Former Maple Leafs general manager Jim Gregory agrees that Williams is a man capable of apparently endless paradox. "I can think of very few hockey players as opinionated as Tiger Williams," says Gregory. "He could drive you crazy with his stubbornness but if you could convince him that a certain course of action was correct and worthwhile, well, nobody would respond with such enthusiasm. He was a guy who could surprise you in a hundred different ways."

For many observing the development of the young hockey player, his most striking quality was a willingness, almost a need, to display loyalty of a remarkable intensity. The fallen coach Red Kelly had been one recipient, in the conflict with Ian Turnbull already mentioned. Williams revered Kelly as a former great player and admired him as a man of dignity, intelligence and compassion. However, Williams is also honest about the fact that his emotional response was so strong on behalf of Kelly because of a sense that he had always been treated considerately by the coach. Of course, Williams was also a practical young man. He had no problem in transferring his loyalty to the new coach, Roger Neilson.

You had to suspect that Red Kelly was a goner when we blew a two-game lead in the series with Philly. That was the kind of thing Harold Ballard just couldn't stomach. He felt a personal humiliation, as though his own manhood had been challenged; when it happened, you knew somebody was going to catch it. At such times Ballard didn't behave too well, and when he got rid of Kelly, he behaved really badly. He cut Kelly down as though he was some Joe Blow who had just walked in off the street. But then, it was nothing to me. I might not approve, I might think that at the very least a Red Kelly was deserving of some respect — and if *he* couldn't get it, there wasn't much hope for poor bastards like me — but Harold Ballard paid the shot. All somebody in my position could do was work and battle, and hope that the new guy liked what he saw. And my luck held with the new guy. I was Roger Neilson's kind of player.

Neilson is the coach who has come closest to telling me that I had a specific job to do on a certain player. As a guy, Neilson is almost a pacifist; but as a coach, they just don't come any tougher. He loves tough players. He acknowledges them, respects them and gives them all the trust in the world. He built his reputation at Peterborough with disciplined teams who were always willing to goon it up in a tight situation, and it seemed that this attitude put a spine in his work. No one ever watched more video, poured himself more fully into the technicalities of the game; but at the end of the day, he never lost sight of the fact that the most vital component of a consistently winning team is character — and the ability to impose real physical strength.

I had first met him at training camp in the fall of 1976, when he was appointed coach of the minor league team in Dallas. He seemed like an interesting, thoughtful guy, and I had a few general conversations with him that seemed as though they might lead to some real insights into the game. He gave me the impression that he had given the game a lot of thought.

Neilson knew exactly what he wanted from somebody like me. When he came to the Leafs, I was coming off a 21-goal

103

year, but he didn't encourage me to have any illusions about being another Mike Bossy. He wanted me to check and scuffle and fight, and he would give me a lot of ice time. I couldn't afford to relax for a second, let alone a shift. I was his kind of player, but he still pointed out my limitations, my lack of some important tools. He said that in many ways I was just what he wanted. I didn't have anything to worry about, as long as I kept my priorities in order.

Red Kelly's device was to talk about carriers of water and choppers of wood. Roger didn't wrap things up. Between periods, sometimes on the bench, he would say things like, "That number 18 seems to be playing pretty well tonight, seems to be doing too much hitting," or, "Number 10 is hitting Borje Salming at will — we shouldn't really be letting him do that." Neilson would never say such things directly to me. But he was always well within my earshot.

Roger also used me in other ways. When he thought a certain player might be low in morale, he would get me to give him a little talk, a little encouragement. I was Neilson's troubleshooter. Darryl Sittler had the public authority and he was a great captain, a classy, fair-minded guy; but there were things I could do that Sittler couldn't. I didn't give a damn as long as we won. Neilson recognized this right away, and you could tell he really approved. He was a really tough son of a bitch. From my point of view, Neilson was exactly what we needed as a coach. He could coach the pants off most guys in the league, and he had no toleration for the floaters. A floater is a guy who looks good when there isn't too much pain involved. We had a few floaters on our team, and I guess the best examples were Ian Turnbull and Errol Thompson.

Ballard thought a lot of Turnbull, and I saw very early that this could be a big problem for Neilson. Turnbull had a lot of natural ability, was quick and smart; but he was a pure rebel, and he wouldn't take anything from anybody, including Ballard. The more Turnbull rebelled, the more Ballard liked him. He didn't work at practice, didn't look after his body. They always made sure that he and I were on the same team in practice because it was well known how much I hated his attitude and how little excuse I would need to get involved in a full-scale fight. The situation was just one of those strange things in the game. Outside of Maple Leaf Gardens, Turnbull

104

impressed me so much. He was smart and amusing, and you had to admit that this was a guy who knew his way around. But inside the rink, I had no use for him at all. At times he could play beautifully, but that only made my feelings towards him even more bitter. I said that as a teammate he was lazy and selfish. I said he was a baby.

It disgusted me that so much talent was being thrown away, and that a coach like Neilson — who spent every waking minute thinking about the game, who sometimes would come to the rink red-eyed because he had been up all night running over film looking for weaknesses in other teams and ways to improve his own — could be wrecked by a guy who couldn't take the trouble to look after himself. And this was a guy who had been given everything needed to be a great player. I would compare his natural ability with mine, how much harder it had been for me to get to this place, and I had to really put a brake on myself because I would get this urge to go out and clobber him, really give him a working over.

Once, I joined Neilson in the sauna at Maple Leaf Gardens and said, "Roger, if you don't get rid of Turnbull he'll get rid of you." I didn't do that lightly. It was a hell of a thing for a player to say to his coach about a teammate, and I remember thinking as I went into the sauna, "Williams, you're putting a goddamned bazooka to your head." I felt I had a responsibility to myself, to guys like Darryl Sittler and Lanny McDonald and to Neilson. But the bizarre thing was that Ballard loved Turnbull; the player who probably could do the most damage to his dream of having a winning team was maybe the most secure member of the club. What I did couldn't really affect the situation in any way, because no matter how Gregory or Neilson felt, neither of them could trade away Turnbull. He was Ballard's man, and when you thought about it for any length of time, you realized that nothing else mattered.

Thompson wasn't in as strong a position as Turnbull, so Neilson traded him — despite the fact that he was a free scorer. Thompson didn't show much on the road, and this meant that I got all the action I needed; I got the chance to show Neilson that it didn't matter to me where I played. Thompson skated like the wind and had a great backhand; and when Hockey Night in Canada was being beamed from Maple Leaf Gardens, it would have taken a team of Clydesdales to hold him back.

But then when we hit the road, he tended to go missing on the ice. It was no good for the team, and it was certainly no good for a coach like Neilson, who wanted to shape everything about the team: the way it operated, the way it drank and slept and, most of all, the way it thought.

Guys like Randy Carlyle and Jack Valiquette had a chance of getting by with a coach like Red Kelly. Red's attitude was that if you did your stuff on the ice, if you didn't make waves, well, he would stick up for you upstairs in the general manager's office and with the press. His message was "Hey, you guys aren't kids, you know what has to be done." This wasn't good enough for Roger Neilson.

Neilson wanted to feel that he had his finger on everything that was happening on the club. He wanted to know about a guy's moods, his mental health as well as his metabolism, and when he said that curfew was eleven o'clock he didn't mean 11:01, and he didn't expect you to make your own decisions about it. Both Carlyle and Valiquette came unstuck with Neilson on trips to Long Island. One night before a game, Neilson knocked on Carlyle's door a few minutes past curfew, found that he wasn't back and decided on the spot that that was the end of Randy Carlyle as a Maple Leaf. A similar incident sent Valiquette to the minors and eventually led to his trade to Colorado. Valiquette hadn't done anything particularly wild, but he was a young guy that got caught, and according to Neilson's rules he had to go.

In that first year or so, Roger Neilson was fanatical about drinking, and I believed it was a necessary phase for the club to go through. Under him, some players had to change their off-ice activities or go; if there was drinking, it was "controlled," at least in theory. If Neilson heard that a player was drinking a little too much, behaving at all erratically, well, that player would get a ticket to the minors or the trading block before he knew what hit him. I believed in Neilson's attitude then and I still do, but looking back, I suspect that maybe he took things a little too far. Randy Carlyle, who was a self-confident guy, deserved what he got, because at that time he was basically a good-time Charlie who never learned to draw the line. However, maybe it should be said that Carlyle went on to become a top defenceman in the NHL and win the Norris Trophy.

Neilson didn't like to see beer around the dressing room. Even back then, it did occur to me that it was probably better for a guy who really wanted a beer to have one or two in the dressing room, because the availability of it there might just take the edge off any urge to go out looking for a drink and a good time. That now seems to me to be the common-sense approach. I also think that maybe Neilson could sometimes lose himself in the game, so that sometimes you sensed he might be getting you to leave too much of your best work on the practice ice. However professional you want to be — and I believe that no one has wanted to be a good pro more than I have — I think you're in trouble if the fun goes out of the game. Neilson's practices were hard, but they were interesting, and you felt they were giving you real assistance in preparing for games. But sometimes they were a little too intense — and sometimes they simply went on too long.

Of course, I'm using hindsight now. Back then I saw Roger Neilson as simply a man who knew what it took to be a winner; a guy who had sat down and figured it all out. He sent us to the University of Waterloo to learn about the human body, to submit ourselves to tests. We were rigged up to machines which told us about our leg strength, our lung capacity and our heart rate. It was a new world for me. Neilson had me talk to Dr. Howie Green and Dr. Mike Houston, who taught me good eating habits and how to monitor the efficiency of my own body. A few years earlier, when I first came to Toronto from Swift Current, I was ignorant of all this. What I had then was just a fierce determination to do all I could to improve myself. I was eager but I had a lot to learn. Now somebody was taking time to show me things, explain why it was better for me to run up mountains rather than jog along the flat. I didn't mind the pain or any of the hardship. I was well trained in hardship. I became the team's guinea pig for various forms of fitness testing. I guess I was like putty in Roger Neilson's hands.

I told Neilson that he should never knock on my door at curfew time. I would take it as an insult. All he had to do was tell me the time I had to be in; he didn't have to check out my integrity. I think he knew that I wasn't making any big promises I would have any problem fulfilling. He knew my character. If I'm going to sit in a bar, I want to take Brenda, my sisters, my brothers, my cousins and all my best friends. I don't want to be in some godforsaken bar in some city I don't know, fending off a bunch of sleezebags and looking over my shoulder to see if anyone is checking up on me. Sittler didn't need that crap. Neither did Ellis. Nor McDonald. I looked around at the guys who needed it and those who didn't, and I knew whose side I was on. There was another point. I don't think I could ever have gone through a game with a hangover. I think I would have broken up out there on the ice. Sometimes in the middle of the summer, I struggle through the day after drinking too much beer the night before. The idea of playing hockey in that condition is just impractical to me. It always surprised me that guys could do it, over and over, and they always seemed to be the guys with the most ability.

The only problem I had with Neilson was that sometimes I used to think he took me for granted. I knew he valued me, that he knew what I could do for him, but there are times when a guy wants something more. Sometimes you want to know that the coach really understands how you tick, and there was a spell at the end of his first year in Toronto when our relationship broke down. At the end of that season, I felt he was really hindering me. When he arrived in Toronto, I was coming off a 21-goal year. To me, playing the way I do, checking, backchecking, fighting, that meant I had had a hell of a good season. Neilson had increased my checking duties and told me that I didn't have to bother about goals. Of course, that's always fine until the club starts looking at your contract and then asks, "How many points did you get?" You don't get asked how tough it is to sit on the bench for fifteen minutes while somebody like Mike Bossy gets plenty of ice time on power plays, and then have to go in and do a job on the son of a bitch, with good timing, sharp judgement.

So I wanted to do my job for the team, but I also wanted to hit that 20-goal mark. We had three games to go at the end of that regular season and I had 19 goals. We had two games at home, then we travelled to Boston to finish the schedule. I hardly got any ice time in the Toronto games. Neilson was experimenting with lines, and I was sitting on the bench — fuming. In Boston I got more time on the ice, naturally, but

Bruins coach Don Cherry seemed to be aware that I was desperate for goal number 20, and he had Terry O'Reilly tight on me all night. I got a couple of chances, once was sent in cold only to hit a post, but I couldn't put the puck in the goddamned net. I went to the dressing room like an old bear with an extremely sore ass.

I tore my equipment off, cursed and stormed off to the team bus without taking a shower. I was convinced that Neilson didn't want me to hit 20 goals, that he didn't want any problems when he told me that he saw me in a purely checking role for the playoffs. He didn't want me to even think goals.

Neilson came up to me later and said, "I hope you're not going to let this affect you in the playoffs." I don't think I'd ever been so mad after a game, and I guess I felt particularly upset because I had come to trust Neilson so much. I said, "Roger, how come you pissed me around so much. I could have got that goal in Toronto and the pressure would have been off me. You knew how important it was to me." He said that the number of goals I scored didn't matter. I was a big player for him, and he was relying on me for the playoffs. If I had a bonus for 20 goals, he would make sure I got it. I said that he was damned right I had a bonus. But in fact, the bonus was small and not too many people at the club realized I was earning as much as $100,000. I wasn't that interested in a couple of thousand in bonus money. I was thinking of my status as a player, my pride; I felt that I had been let down in a way that I couldn't easily pinpoint.

But then, it was a brief crisis. When the playoffs came, the hurt had gone. I sensed that as a team we were getting close to being truly competitive at the highest level. As a team, Philadelphia were further down the road, had greater understanding; and Montreal undoubtedly had more talent. But under Neilson we had a growing ambition. He taxed us in ways beyond the ability of Red Kelly, and on the bench his brain seemed to work like a computer.

By the spring of 1978 we were so close we could taste the Stanley Cup. We rolled over Los Angeles in the first round and then beat out the Islanders four games to three. Against the

Islanders, Roger Neilson gave a classic lesson on the value of a good coach. The team was perfectly prepared, mentally and physically. Neilson had me as a full-time checker, but I also got to work on the power play, a power play that had become the best in the league. When we had the man advantage, I would play in front of the net — it was a time when you really paid a price for doing that; after each game, my back was covered in welts — with Sittler and McDonald on either side. Salming and Turnbull would shoot the puck from the points. Even though Salming was injured in the first game and put out for the rest of the series, we still produced.

Our series with the Islanders was real hockey — the best I've ever played in. We lost the first two games on the Island, but Neilson never allowed us to think in terms of defeat. On the flight back from New York, he came to me and said, "Make sure nobody's down. We're very close, we can take this team." A lot of coaches say things like that in a desperate effort to get something going, but with Roger it was convincing. In the games in Toronto, we attacked the Islanders physically and with the puck. Boutette speared Bossy, and so did I; and Jerry Butler hit him with a beautiful check that appeared to knock him out. The New York players went crazy when Butler hit Bossy, who was taken off to hospital. I said that there didn't seem to be anything wrong with Bossy, except that maybe his heart had given out. As a team, we had really got inside the Islanders, knocked them off their stride, agitated them. Clark Gillies took a terrific run at me at centre, missed, and crashed into Bryan Trottier. The collision broke Trottier's jaw. The little guy had his jaw wired up and came back, but even a Trottier is going to be affected by something like that. Bob Nystrom and I fought several times. Once, he bit me so badly on the cheek that I needed nine stitches — five for his top teeth, four for the bottom. (Paul Holmgren once bit me and I didn't get any stitches: he bit a hunk out of my back, and the doctor said he couldn't stitch the wound.)

There are times in a series when you know you have the other team, that something has gone out of them. If you had to pick a moment when the balance of power changed in that Islander series, it was probably the moment Butler smacked into Bossy. We were sharp in every department, and the longer the series went the more assured we became.

Even so, the seventh game became an agony for me in the third period. I jostled Gerry Hart in front of the Islanders goal and knocked him down, and the referee gave me a penalty. I couldn't believe a referee would call such a cheap penalty in the third period of a seventh game, and I screamed at him before charging down the ice and crashing into Lorne Henning. I got two minutes for tripping Hart, two minutes for roughing Henning. The game was tied when I got the penalties. Those four minutes in the penalty box seemed like four years. I had twenty-three million people saying that that asshole Williams just blew the series.

I thought of my dad back home in Weyburn, sitting in front of the television and possibly having a heart attack. Normally I never worried about taking penalties; it was my style of play, it was approved by the coach, and there was no doubt it gave us plenty of momentum and an edge. A lot of guys in the league just couldn't figure out where I was coming from. It was also true that we had great penalty-killing. On this occasion, Jimmy Jones and Jerry Butler were magnificent. Turnbull had had a terrible year, but now he was playing beautifully. For me, leaving the penalty box with the game still tied was like leaving a death cell. The game went into overtime, and Lanny McDonald got the series winner. He took the puck off the end of my stick and drilled it past Chico Resch.

We beat the Islanders, who had more talent than we did, because Roger Neilson coached the series brilliantly. He never let up for a second, working the bench, prodding the players, drawing the best out of every one of us. Every night we came to play; every shift we gave the sons of bitches a little more pressure. In the semi-finals against Montreal, it was obvious Neilson had taken us as far as we could go. They checked the crap out of us, and when you added it all up, they just had too many great players.

I missed the second and third games with an injury and came back for the fourth — we were down 3–0 — with a knee brace. After that fourth game, Scotty Bowman shook my hand and said, "You're a gutsy player — a lot of guys wouldn't have come back injured with their team three games down." But I didn't have good feelings for Bowman. He was always whining to officials; you could hear him on the bench. When he paid me the compliment, I looked into his eyes and said, "I wanted to beat you."

A year later, it was the same story with the Canadiens — they were still too good for us. Again they beat us four straight, this time in the quarter-finals. I didn't like Bowman, but he was obviously a great coach, and he had wonderful raw material: Lafleur and Robinson, Savard and Dryden; well, those guys were just awesome. In what proved to be the last game of the series, Larry Robinson did me one of the biggest favours of my life. I wouldn't have needed the favour if it hadn't been for a horseshit call by the referee, Bob Myers, in overtime. Myers called a high-sticking penalty against me, and I paid the full price — it cost us the game. Robinson, the man I was supposed to have high-sticked, scored the winning goal. On the penalty, there is no doubt my stick was up, but it wasn't over the boards, and for me to high-stick Robinson I would have needed a frigging ladder.

When I came out of the box as the game ended, I just went for Myers. I wanted to kill the son of a bitch. Robinson must have seen something in my eyes, because he headed right for me and grabbed me; only a guy as big, strong and fast as Robinson could have done it. He wrapped his big arms around me and said, "Forget it, kid, it was a horseshit call, but I'll take you fishing in the summer." The big guy saved my neck all right, because if I'd got hold of Myers, I'm sure I would have done him serious damage.

In the dressing room I cried. I'd never done that before — and I haven't done it since. Quite a few of the guys came up to me and said, "Hey, don't worry, we weren't going to win the goddamned series, anyway." But that didn't impress me. In the previous game, we had taken them to overtime, and they only won because Cam Connor got a freak goal. Connor lost the puck in front of our goal, fell down and then watched the puck trickle over the line. Mike Palmateer said, "That's one thing I can't do — defend against a guy who doesn't know what he's doing." If Connor hadn't got that goal, if Myers hadn't given that horseshit penalty . . . Who knows? We might have got some momentum — it's the kind of thinking you really shouldn't indulge in, but I couldn't shake it that night.

When the dressing room had cleared, Roger Neilson came up to me and said, "Don't worry about that. I know it's hard to take, but that was the worst call I've ever seen. You play your guts out and we need you. Whatever you do, don't kill yourself."

Sometimes I'm asked within the game why I always stick up for Neilson despite the fact that he has given me all the shitty jobs, and I try to explain that it is a mixture of things. But mostly it is because of nights like that one in Maple Leaf Gardens. You always try to make out that you're the toughest son of a bitch who ever drew breath, but sometimes you need a guy like Roger Neilson to come along and say, "Hey, don't worry, you're okay." And Roger always knows when to say that.

It was Neilson who got me to sign a new contract with the Leafs at a time when I knew I could make a financial killing in New York or maybe Detroit. Both John Ferguson of the Rangers and Ted Lindsay of the Red Wings made it clear that they could use me, and I understood that Ferguson was ready to give me a good contract for two years with a one-year option. I always said I would never have my kids growing up in New York City. To me the place was a jungle filled with mad dogs. Now I know that you can live outside Manhattan and that if you do well on the ice, New York can be a hell of a place to operate for a few years.

But what did I really want with New York City? I was a Canadian who loved Canada. I had a good coach, and I played on what I thought was one of the best lines in the game. I had Sittler and McDonald and Neilson, and I could sit in Ungerman's office with the big shots. Who needed more? So I signed up for another six years with the Leafs. By the end of those years, I would have fulfilled my ambition to play ten years in the National Hockey League. The only trouble was that I signed too cheaply — $125,000 a year — and that in the battle between Ian Turnbull and Roger Neilson, Turnbull was winning, thanks to Harold Ballard's support.

Roger Neilson was fired in the middle of the 1978–79 season. He got the word that he was probably gone when we flew into Montreal. Before the game he seemed quite emotional, and he said to us, "Guys, I think this is going to be my last game with you. I want you to do one thing for me. I want you to play like you did against the Islanders. I want you to play it my way."

We did the best we could; we played well even though we lost

113

a great game 4–3. On the flight home to Toronto, we filled in a questionnaire Roger had prepared back in his hotel room. He wanted us to rate him on various aspects of the job: communication, practice, line changing. He said we shouldn't sign our names. He just wanted to get a better idea of where he had gone wrong. I urged the guys to fill in the questionnaire as fully as they could, because here was a coach who wasn't whining when he got canned. He wanted to improve himself, and I was very impressed. Back at the Gardens, Roger had a word with each of the players. Some of the guys had two seconds with him, some a lot longer. I was the last to see him; I wanted it to be that way. He seemed worn out, so I suggested that we go get something to eat in the Hot Stove, the restaurant at the Gardens. This restaurant is something of an institution in the game. Directors of the club used to eat there regularly.

Over lunch I asked Neilson, "If Ballard asked you back, would you come?"

Neilson said, "Of course — I like the team and I think it's very close to real success. Also I'm unemployed."

I raced home and got on the telephone. First I called Sittler and asked him how he felt about Neilson's departure. He said that he was disappointed; the club didn't have anyone to replace him and the playoffs were coming up. We agreed to poll all the players, get them to the rink at nine o'clock the following morning and take a vote. If the vote was overwhelming, Sittler would go to Ballard as team captain. The vote was about ninety per cent in Neilson's favour. One of the few to go against him was Turnbull. According to Sittler, when he asked Turnbull if he would vote for Neilson's re-instatement, Turnbull said, "No way."

Sittler went up to Ballard's office and told him about the team's vote. Ballard came to meet us, listened to Sittler, who could be very eloquent, saying that Neilson had the team's respect and that whatever had gone wrong was the fault of the players. Ballard said, "Okay, you've got your coach back, but you bastards better make sure you start to do something."

Then he walked out of the room and slammed the door.

I didn't get involved in any of the other business to do with Neilson's re-instatement. I don't know why Ballard suggested that Neilson return to the bench wearing a paper bag over his head, other than to get the cheapest kind of publicity. But I felt proud that I had been able to change the course of events and have a certain influence with the rest of the team. I had fought for a man I believed in, helped to give him a second chance he richly deserved.

It was a shame we couldn't go on to win the Stanley Cup. It was an even greater shame when Neilson was gonged again that summer. Ballard brought in Punch Imlach, and that was more than a shame. That was a goddamned tragedy.

11

To Dave Williams, the news of George "Punch" Imlach's appointment as general manager of the Maple Leafs in the summer of 1979 was stunning. He had met Imlach only once, briefly. It was a chance encounter on Yonge Street in his second year with Toronto. Williams was then an emerging celebrity; Imlach had won four Stanley Cups as coach and manager of the Leafs in the 1960s. Recognizing Imlach, Williams introduced himself. In response, Imlach's manner seemed both stiff and cool. Then, Williams had shrugged: Imlach was hockey history. Now, Punch Imlach was Tiger Williams's new boss.

Imlach's talent for assembling a winning team, at least on a short-term basis, was in the record book, but since losing his job in Buffalo, he had been on the fringes of the game. He had tried his hand at writing, with a syndicated newspaper column. Dave Williams had read some of the columns and had concluded from the views expressed in them that Imlach was rooted in the past. Williams thought the writer's perceptions were shaped by old triumphs and that his responses were geared to a bygone age, a time when players gratefully accepted their paycheques and did not hire high-powered lawyers as their agents or discuss such concepts as "player power."

Williams saw clearly that the new general manager, and his coach, Floyd Smith, would oppose what to Williams was the best influence in the Maple Leaf dressing room. This influence was the block of opinion led by the talented and articulate stars of the team, Darryl Sittler — the captain — and Lanny McDonald, the dignified but also charismatic scorer. Both of these players were represented by Toronto lawyer Alan Eagleson, who, in the eyes of Imlach — and Harold Ballard — was quickly eroding the old power of the owners and general managers. Williams, a fierce protector of Sittler and McDonald on the ice, and a warm, admiring friend off it, felt himself being drawn into a conflict that would rip the club apart.

Before the end of that year, Williams's worst fears were confirmed. Lanny McDonald was traded to Colorado in early December, and soon afterwards, just before a game at Maple Leaf Gardens, Williams came upon Sittler in a back room removing the captain's C from his jersey. Beside Sittler was a statement printed in block letters on his personal stationery, which had his team number 27 imprinted on a Maple Leaf. Sittler showed Williams the statement and told him that he would be reading it to the press after the game. (Imlach would later charge that Sittler's actions were not as spontaneous as many people, including Williams, believed.)

Williams read, "I told my team-mates and my coach before the game that I was resigning as captain of the Toronto Maple Leafs. When I was made captain it was the happiest day of my life. I have tried to handle my duties as captain in an honest and fair manner. I took player complaints to management and discussed management ideas with players.

"At the start of this season, I was personally sued by my own hockey team management. I was told it was nothing personal. I explained my position to Mr. Imlach and Mr. Ballard at that time. I told them that I felt a captain's role was to work with players and management, not just management. Mr. Ballard and Mr. Imlach made some negative comments about me and my team-mates some weeks ago and I met with them to discuss it. I was told I was being too sensitive. I have had little or no contact with Mr. Imlach and it is clear to me that he and I have different ideas about player and management communication. I have recently been told that management has prevented me from appearing on Hockey Night in Canada telecasts. I am spending more and more time on player-management problems and I don't feel I am accomplishing enough for my team-mates. The "war" between Mr. Imlach and Mr. Eagleson should not overshadow the main issue — Toronto Maple Loafo.

"I am totally loyal to the Toronto Maple Leafs. I don't want to let my team-mates down but I have to be honest with myself. I will continue to

117

fight for players' rights, but not as captain of the team. All I want to do is give all my energy and all my ability to my team as a player."

To the public, Sittler's statement was just another round of hockey politics. To Dave Williams, it signalled the end of his most hopeful days as a hockey player.

With Sittler at war and Lanny McDonald suddenly gone — to goddamned Colorado of all places — it was as though someone had come in off the street and pulled down the walls of my house. I used to think that McDonald, Sittler and me had everything. McDonald shot the puck like a rocket. Sittler could do everything in a way that was well above average. And I could stir up the shit, knock 'em down and drag 'em out. Whenever I took a bad penalty, Darryl would skate by and say, "Okay, okay"; he gave me all the reassurance in the world. If he had any criticism, it would always be constructive. Sometimes he might say to me, "Gee, maybe you should have waited just a little in that situation." But he never cut me down. He, McDonald and I were like the three frigging muskateers. Under Neilson, we used to have those hard practices and then do speed skating, and that was often a bit of a crisis for me. Sittler would come alongside me and say, "Now keep up, kid, keep up." He would give me a little tap with his stick. He was always rooting for me, and it was one of the best things that ever happened to me on the ice.

I hear stories now that Lanny McDonald is, well, a little bit disenchanted with me, and it may be so. We've had some big battles since the Calgary–Vancouver series built up into a real rivalry, and I've always tried to make his life miserable as a Calgary player. But I can't believe his resentment goes that deep. He knows that when we were teammates, nobody could have done more for him than I did; no one else could have looked after him so closely. It was part of that deal which is sometimes struck up between players, without really being stated. It just grows. It is made up of self-interest to some degree but mostly of respect. I admired McDonald as a player and as a man, and when our line was first formed, I said to both him and Sittler, "Look guys, I'll look after all the bullshit, all the fighting. I'll do the back-checking, all the heavy work. You guys just have to score. That way they've got to keep us

118

together." Sittler and McDonald never let me down. They were great guys.

At the worst of the fighting, Sittler sometimes would say, "Hey, you just have to quit all this fighting at this level — in another year, your hands are going to be like raw meat. You're just doing too much of it." Sittler had character like iron. He was right up there with Lafleur and Robinson and Dryden; he was a household name, but he never took anything for granted. He never took his success for granted, nor the people around him. Often he would turn down a commercial and steer it in my direction. Usually it would be worth around $500, which was a useful sum in those days.

When McDonald got traded early in December, 1979, it was like a punch in the face for both Sittler and me. In fact, the reaction throughout the dressing room was one of the most emotional things I've ever seen. McDonald walked into the room after the game with a piece of paper in his hand. It was like a pink slip when a worker gets dumped from a job, and it had his flight times typed on it. He didn't say anything. He just handed the piece of paper to Sittler, who read it, then started crying. When it was clear that McDonald was on his way, other guys started to cry. It was really unbelievable. The guys who weren't into crying started throwing things around. Just off the dressing room is a room where the guys used to shave after a game. Somebody hurled cans of shaving cream all over the place. For about five minutes, we just went on a rampage. The whole goddamned club was breaking up, it seemed.

Rocky Saganiuk, a cockie rookie, said that he would replace McDonald. We were all pissed off with him. A few days later in Winnipeg, after practice we shaved him completely, strapped him to a treatment table and pushed him out on the ice and left him there.

Yeah, we were shocked when Lanny McDonald was traded — for Wilf Paiement and Pat Hickey — but by this time everyone knew that changes had become inevitable. Right from the start, Imlach had created a new, harsh atmosphere in the Gardens. It was as though we were stepping back in time. One of the first things he did was impose a very tough dress code. According to Imlach, it was wrong to leave your hotel room without wearing a jacket and tie, even if you just wanted to go

119

to the gift shop for a newspaper or magazine. And no one was allowed to go into Imlach's office without a tie.

Once, I had to go to see Ballard, who had no dress code regulations. I wasn't wearing a tie. Imlach saw me leaving Ballard's office and he shouted, "Hey, Williams, what are you doing without a tie?" I said I wasn't aware that I needed one to visit Ballard. Imlach fined me $150. It was a typical Imlach touch — petty, insulting. He treated us all like children.

Early in his regime, the coach, Floyd Smith, came into the dressing room after practice — which in Toronto was held at 10:30 A.M. religiously — and told us we were all expected back at 3:00 P.M. to look at game film. One of the guys said, "Hey, Smithy, we're going to get caught in rush hour," and Smith just snapped, "That's the way it is, don't talk to me." It was obvious that Smith just did what Imlach told him. The guys decided to wreck the film session. Turnbull produced a pornographic film and put it on the machine. I'd taken the game film and hidden it behind some boxes beside the projector. When Smith turned on the film and took a look at what was on the screen, he cancelled the session, and we all broke up.

Some of the things Imlach imposed were bizarre — like the time he had the icemakers at the Gardens draw red lines parallel to the boards about fifteen feet from them. In the practice, the wingers were told to keep outside the red lines, and centres had to stay inside them. It was prehistoric hockey, and sometimes when I think about it now, I have to laugh. I try to imagine what Gretzky and Anderson and Messier would have said if they had been told to skate without crossing over those red lines. Imlach also had the dressing room phone yanked out; he didn't give any reason for doing it. Anybody could see that he wanted confrontations. He wanted to pick off the main men, and we all knew that it was only a matter of time. We were like guys in the trenches just waiting to be hit by a sniper.

Even before McDonald was traded, an incident took place that told you all you wanted to know about the state of Imlach's relations with the majority of the players. We were gathering at the Toronto airport in November to catch a plane to Montreal for a game there. As we were getting out of our cars, someone noticed that Imlach had left his lights on. Somebody else said, "Don't tell the bastard, piss on it." We couldn't wait to get back to Toronto. When we returned, we all sat in our cars waiting to hear the dead splutter from Imlach's car. Then we all roared our engines. Carl Brewer was travelling with Imlach, and he rushed around asking guys for a jump-start. They all said they didn't have any booster cables. Dave Hutchison had a souped-up Corvette. He pulled up alongside Imlach and waved a set of booster cables out the window. Then he roared away laughing.

After that, I guess it was a question of who would go first. Hutchison for waving the booster cables? Sittler and McDonald for being Eagleson men? Me for being a pal of Sittler and McDonald's. It was a sick hockey club, and the thing that made you bitter was to think how close we'd come to being a real team. Under Neilson we had always been beaten out by the eventual Stanley Cup champions. And our closeness as team-mates was something a new guy should have gloried in. Instead, Imlach wanted to break us up.

Sittler would have been the first to go, but he had a no-trade clause in his contract, so all Imlach could do was give him pinpricks or get at him through others like McDonald. One of the first little jabs at Sittler was a refusal to allow him to appear on the Hockey Night in Canada feature, "Showdown." Imlach had the idea that "Showdown", which had the league's best shooters going against the top goaltenders and offered a first prize of $15,000, was an Eagleson product, and by now he was absolutely paranoid about hockey agents, especially Alan Eagleson. Older guys have told me that back in the sixties Imlach was a great coach. They say he got very close to his players and always looked after them. But that doesn't square with my experience. To me it seemed that Imlach was only happy if he had a real grip on all the players, like a sergeant major rather than a hockey man. He wanted everybody to jump to attention.

Imlach wasn't the only one bothered by Alan Eagleson. Another was Harold Ballard. In fact, McDonald was moved to Colorado in the middle of a bitter battle between Ballard and Eagleson. It concerned a proposed game between the Maple Leafs and the Canadian Olympic team preparing for the Lake Placid Winter Games. The stupid thing was that the issue didn't really involve Eagleson. He got drawn into it by Imlach, who was practically frothing at the mouth whenever Eagleson's name was mentioned.

We had played the Olympic team in a pre-season contest in Calgary, and the game had been a complete disaster. Ballard had insisted we go in without our best players: Salming, Sittler and McDonald. I captained the team. The kids on the Olympic team had nothing to lose, and they played well. They were leading by about three goals when some of our guys started to get pissed off. Before the game, we had agreed that we would go easy on the kids — soon they would be representing Canada in the Olympics, and we had to do our bit to help. Unfortunately all the good resolutions went up in smoke when the Olympic team got a little cocky. You couldn't blame the kids. They were doing well against an experienced professional team. But some of our guys got uptight with the situation and started taking runs at the kids. On one shift we were really pounding them, and I skated over to the Olympic team's bench and said to the coach, Tom Watt, "For God's sake, Tom, you gotta do something! Clear the benches." But Watt refused; he said he was teaching his boys discipline.

The business in Calgary was at the back of most players' minds when we heard that Ballard had agreed to play another game at the Gardens in December. George Cohan, head of McDonald's in Canada, had proposed that the game be played on behalf of both the Olympic team and the Ronald McDonald House charity. McDonald's would buy up the house, Ballard would donate the building — and get a tax write-off — and Canada's hockey team and a worthwhile charity would benefit. Cohan mentioned the game during a business conversation with Eagleson, who said, "Hey, wait a minute, did anyone mention this to the players?"

It was a good question, because the game was to take place in the middle of the heaviest part of our schedule, at a time when we knew we had a fight on to beat out Minnesota for a playoff spot. We had games against Minnesota, Buffalo and Boston in a five-day period, and the management was proposing to drop in the Olympic team game. We read about the proposal in the press, and the reaction in the dressing room was really hostile. At that time, we were having a lot of problems with morale; we were struggling to get a position in the league, and suddenly we were being asked to play four games in five days. Nobody wanted to spoil a charity effort, but there were some other principles involved. Ballard was getting his tax write-off and good publicity, and McDonalds' would also draw a huge benefit in publicity. The only people who didn't stand to gain anything were the players on the Toronto Maple Leafs, and we were the only ones not consulted.

A deputation of players went to Ballard to say that we would co-operate with the club in any way we could, but this proposal was ridiculous. We would play a charity game at a more suitable time. We pointed out that we were always available for charity work but that we were also professionals. We said we were being asked to go into a no-win situation, and considering the time of season — and especially the way the game in Calgary had gone — the whole thing was crazy. Ballard said that Eagleson was putting us up to a rebellion. It was true that several of us were at that time slipping over to the Westbury Hotel to meet Eagleson, but such meetings were not his idea. Through his clients Sittler and McDonald, we had asked Eagleson for help. We felt that we needed someone to look out for us as a group.

One compromise suggestion which appealed to me was that if we played this game, Ballard would lift his ban on Russian hockey teams appearing at Maple Leaf Gardens. Back in Junior days, I had been selected to join an Edmonton Oil Kings all-star team to meet the Russians, but on the day of the game, the Edmonton owner, "Wild" Bill Hunter, had cut me. It was an old wound that often flared up from time to time, and now I said, "Hell, let's get that game on — I want to play against those Russian bastards." But when Ballard heard our proposal, he just told us to go to hell.

Eventually Ballard and Imlach were standing up front at a press conference in the Hot Stove. The announcement of the Olympic game was made, and there was quite a bit of bullshit flying around. Lanny McDonald, as the players' association representative, stepped out of the crowd and walked up to the microphone. He said, "I'm sorry, but we're not playing this game." You could have heard a pin drop in that room. I guess it was a declaration of war, and I guess all the sports media in Toronto got their first clear view of the head of the pimple. And you didn't have to be too smart to see that it was a juicy bastard.

Looking back, the issues seem quite simple. The players were saying, "Look, you've been horsing us around for too long.

123

You've brought in this guy Imlach, who is so full of ego and what he did yesterday that he can't see what's before his eyes." We were saying that we had had enough.

Sittler was a class guy and he was being treated like dirt. McDonald was a player who could score 50 goals when it was a hell of a challenge, and Imlach schemed him down to the dead men in Colorado. It made your stomach turn when you thought of what was happening to a team that might just have made it in a city which was screaming for success.

Hickey, who had been part of the McDonald trade, said to me later, "Why do you hate me?" and I replied, "I don't hate you. I just think you're a goddamned floater." I had nothing against Hickey as a guy, but I couldn't get it out of my mind that he was part of the McDonald deal. I guess it stuck in my throat.

When I spoke so bitterly to Hickey, I already knew I was history as far as Toronto was concerned. I thought about the way they had treated Lanny McDonald. He had bought a new house in Mississauga just a few days before he was traded to Denver. I made up my mind that I wasn't going to just sit and wait until something like that happened to me. I wasn't going to let Imlach take his time, then move me to Pittsburgh or some other godforsaken, no-hope outfit. I called Herb Pinder and said that I had my old ear to the rail and could hear the train coming. It was only a matter of time before it got me. I asked him to do some fishing around. I told him I hated the idea of getting dumped by Imlach. I wanted to try to control my own destiny.

Pinder asked me which clubs I liked, and I told him my short list. I'd always enjoyed Chicago Stadium, and I'd had a feeling for the Windy City ever since my honeymoon. I also liked Boston. I liked the feel of the old place and the atmosphere in Boston Garden. I always thought it was conducive to the game, despite the presence of Wayne Cashman. And there was Vancouver, a beautiful city when it stopped raining, I had always been told.

I had some contacts in Vancouver. Dave Dunn had been a teammate in Toronto and was now assistant coach of the Canucks. Jake Milford, the general manager, had hitched a ride on the Swift Current iron lung back in my Junior days and

I had had a good conversation with him. Vancouver might be a perfect jumping off point. When we played the Canucks, I had a word with Dunn. I told him that I was history as far as Imlach was concerned, but I felt I could make a contribution to the Canucks. They seemed to have some talent, but in a lot of games they didn't seem to be that well motivated. Maybe I had something they could use. A few days later, Milford called Pinder and said that he was ready to trade for me, but he wanted to know my terms. Pinder told him I had four years left on my Toronto contract and Vancouver could take it over. It was left there. I had put out some feelers, and I just had to wait for something to happen. I was preparing for the moment when I would leave Toronto, though I knew that when the moment came, it would still be a shock.

Early in February 1980 we were playing in Madison Square Garden, and I got a kind of premonition that this would be my last night in a Maple Leaf jersey. I remember turning to Dave "Bunky" Burrows as we sat in the dressing room between periods. I said to Burrows, who was a good defenceman even though he had a body like a rack of bones, "Bunky, this is my last game. I can feel it." Burrows said that I was talking bullshit, but I was convinced and I told a few other guys, including Sittler. I had been roomed with Jerry Butler, which was unusual. I wondered if we were both on our way. At that point in the season I had 21 goals, which equalled my previous best, and because I felt so sure I was leaving, I said that I would love to score in the Garden that night. The game was close, and the Rangers pulled their goalie to try for a tie. With three seconds left, Sittler slid me the puck. All I had to do was just jab it into the empty net. I said, "Thanks Sitt" — for the last time, as things turned out.

After the game, we travelled to the Holiday Inn in Uniondale, where we were to play the Islanders. Borje Salming had a Swedish pal based in Manhattan, and he arranged for a limousine to pick up some of the guys for a night on the town. It involved the breaking of club rules, and so it was something that I couldn't do myself, even though I was disgusted by the way Imlach was treating us. I warned the guys that they were still getting paid by the club and that Imlach was the kind of guy who could just blow up. I didn't think he would mind slapping suspensions on guys and denying wages. But by this

125

stage, there was a lot of mutiny in the air, and the theory which won the night was that there was safety in numbers.

My new roommate, Butler, said that he was going to take the trip and have a few drinks. I told him that on this occasion I wouldn't have any problem holding the fort, covering for him. He was a good, responsible guy who worked like a bastard for the club, and, like all of us, he was feeling pissed off by the situation. He wanted a break. It wasn't as though he was some floater who was only interested in a good time.

When the guys left for Manhattan, I went with a few stragglers for a late dinner in a Chinese place just down the block. Over the meal, I returned to the theme that I was gone, and when there was some more disagreement, I said, "If I'm still here at the end of the week, I'll pay for everyone's meal."

It was around 1:45 A.M. when I returned to the hotel. I was walking down the corridor towards my room when Dick Duff, who by then was an Imlach puppet, came up to me and handed me an envelope. He said, "You got traded." Inside the envelope there was an air ticket to Toronto. I asked Duff where I was going. He said, "I can't say." I asked him where the coach was. He said he didn't know. But he volunteered the information that Imlach was in the bar. I went into the bar and found Imlach sitting at a table in a dark corner. I asked him where I was being sent. At first he refused to tell me anything beyond the fact that Butler was going with me. Eventually he said that the club was Vancouver but I couldn't tell anyone at this point. I learned later that the secrecy was at Vancouver's insistence. Rick Vaive and Billy Derlago, who were coming to the Maple Leafs, were out on the town, and nobody in Vancouver could get hold of them.

I had a few things to say to Punch Imlach, and this was a good time to say them. I told him that I could get along with anyone in the world if I wanted to, and that I could also be the biggest jerk in the world when I wanted to be. But I had done everything I could for the Maple Leafs and for him as a boss. This was because I was a professional and also because I felt a debt to Harold Ballard and King Clancy, and I knew those old guys had been counting on me at a difficult time in the club's life. I had gone through life trying not to let people down, but Imlach was something else. I said that the McDonald trade was garbage and that Sittler was one of the best leaders the game

126

had to offer. I said that maybe Punch Imlach was once a great hockey man, but it had gone now. I leaned across the table and said, "Punch, you've lost it, boy."

Imlach went crazy when I said those things. He started pounding the table. He said that he had been the last guy to bring the Stanley Cup to Maple Leaf Gardens, and he was the only man in the world who could bring it back. He said that the club and the players were nothing without him, and I'd better tell the guys before I left that it was going to be his way or the highway. I said that he should take a real good look at the situation and get rid of all the bullshit or else make way for somebody who would.

I went back to my room and called Brenda. I didn't get any sleep that night and it took me quite a time to convince Jerry Butler that he was also heading to the West Coast. Imlach left the hotel before Butler could talk to him. Butler then asked Smith about his status, and Smith said he didn't know what was going on. We got a taxi to La Guardia airport and flew back to Toronto, where we were booked first class to Vancouver. In Toronto the reporters came after us, wanting us to talk about Imlach. We said, "No comment."

Brenda was visiting her folks in Swift Current, so I returned to an empty house to pack some clothes for the trip to Vancouver. On the way back to Toronto airport, Butler said, "For your sake, Williams, it better be true that I'm traded." He still hadn't had the trade confirmed by an official of the Maple Leafs. He was a good guy, Butsy. He played his guts out for the Maple Leafs. And nobody even bothered to say goodbye.

12

There was hurt and anger in Dave Williams on the long flight to Vancouver. But mostly there was defiance. He would show Punch Imlach that his assessment of hockey players was deeply flawed. He would show his old mentor Harold Ballard that it was a bad day for the Toronto Maple Leafs when the youthful talents of a Rick Vaive and a Billy Derlago were rated above the warrior intensity of a Tiger Williams.

Williams had been banished from a place he had come to love for its sense of importance and a certain vitality. However pretentious some aspects of Toronto life, Williams would always see the city as the embodiment of one of his greatest goals. For him, and vividly, Toronto had come to represent the big time. He was hurt that his beloved King Clancy had not said goodbye, and it was soothing to hear later that the great man had been upset by the news of Williams's departure, so upset that he had avoided a farewell scene. Such sentiment was important to Williams.

Dave Williams had once called at the home of Conn Smythe, rather as a pilgrim might visit a shrine. He explained to Smythe how much he wanted to make a contribution to the Maple Leafs and that the best of the great club's tradition seemed to revolve around the name Conn Smythe. Smythe was favourably impressed by the young man. When Smythe died, Williams insisted on attending the funeral, breaking away

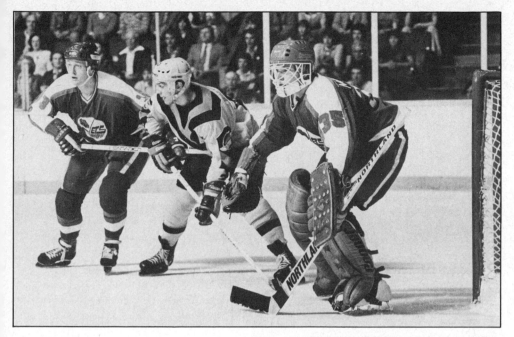

The most valuable chore . . . bringing
confusion to the slot.

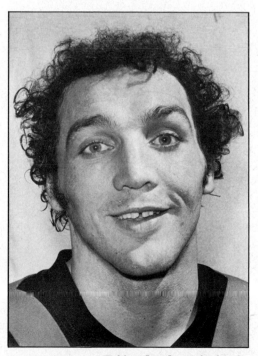

Taking five from the battle.
(Bill Cunningham)

Take that, Willie Huber! (Bill Cunningham)

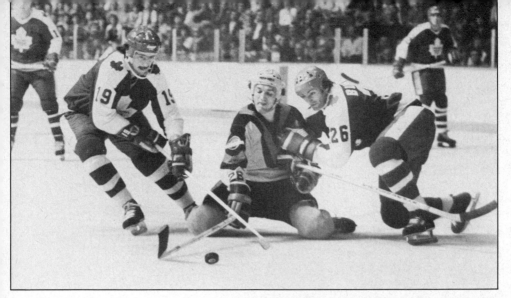

Beating the Leafs. Canuck Williams puts it all
in against his old team. (Bill Cunningham)

The Tiger's stride. (S. R. Smith)

Signing autographs at a club
charity baseball game.
(Bill Cunningham)

Williams rides his sword in triumph, his usual
response to a goal. (Graig Abel)

Williams and friend after a practice session. Zetta Dalby Kendall celebrated her hundredth birthday with a visit to her favourite hockey player. (*The Sun*, Vancouver)

Tiger Williams and friends from the Special Olympics. (Bill Cunningham)

The scoring touch . . . Williams deceives
Winnipeg goalie Doug Soetaert. (Bill
Cunningham)

Going for the Cup . . . Williams loses balance
but wins a vital game over Calgary in overtime.
(Bill Cunningham)

Tiger Williams and Billie Smith, men hard to
separate on the ice. (Bill Cunningham)

from the Vancouver team, which was then on the road in Hartford. To make up for the fact that he was missing practice, Williams took a strenuous run along the shores of Lake Ontario before attending the funeral. It was bitingly cold on the lakeshore, and Williams ran too far. In the Hartford game, he played poorly and received some cutting criticism from coach Harry Neale.

Williams was unrepentant. He would always give his best for whoever paid his wages, but there were some things, some spiritual things, that transcended all other considerations. When he went to Conn Smythe's funeral, he was making a personal statement about his life and his attitude to hockey. To some of the Vancouver players, it seemed a quirkish gesture. But it scarcely surprised them. They had quickly seen that Williams marched to his own drummer. And sometimes the beat could be erratic — at least to those who did not share his extraordinary compulsion to win.

Right from the start, there was a certain friction between some of the Vancouver guys and me, and it came to the surface in a bizarre way at the end of the season, which I'll talk about later. Almost from the first moment I walked into the dressing room in February 1980 I noticed that the general attitude was different from mine.

That was quite a moment for me, walking into a new dressing room after more than five years in Maple Leaf Gardens. Butler was an old hand. He had been through the St. Louis and New York Rangers organizations before arriving in Toronto. I asked Butler for the scoop on how you introduced yourself to new teammates. He seemed a little surprised by the question and said, "Do what the hell you like." So I just marched into the dressing room and introduced myself to everyone, telling them who I was and what I was going to do for the club, and all that bullshit. Butler should have told me that the thing to do was just go into the damned place, sit down and wait for them to come to you.

Maybe I got off on the wrong foot, but that wasn't the source of the problem. It was caused by the difference in attitude. There were some talented players on the Canucks, but the team's attitude was bad. In fact, you could say the attitude was horseshit. The older players just didn't seem to want to lead. It was too early to say what the reason was. Maybe they hadn't been treated very well by the management, maybe they had

129

never known what it was to be a winner; anyway, they didn't seem to appreciate my approach, which had always been the same. I believed that it didn't matter how old you were — whether you were a rookie or a guy in his tenth year, you had to go out and give it everything you had. I formed the impression that a lot of guys had decided they were going to take a free ride. They didn't have to worry about getting the level of media abuse I was used to in Toronto when things didn't work out well in a game.

My first game for the Canucks, against St. Louis, was so important to me. I wanted to make the big impact. The Pacific Coliseum was sold out, for the first time that season. Unfortunately I had caught some bug in New York and the plane trip didn't help. Then in Vancouver we had a heavy workout on the day of the game and I wasn't used to that. But none of this mattered once the game started. I tried my damnedest to score, but it didn't work out. On my first shift I hit the goal post, and that's as close as I came. The fact is that I didn't play very well, but I did the best I could on that particular night. What bothered me the most was that I didn't think you could say the same for the whole team.

The game only strengthened my first impressions of the Vancouver Canucks. On the negative side was the bad attitude among the players; on the positive side was the fact that the management appeared to be aware of it. Harry Neale and his assistant Dave Dunn seemed to be attacking the problem as best they could. I guess a lot of guys in my position would have held off, been a little neutral about the situation, but that wasn't my way; and soon enough I realized I had gotten on the wrong side of about half the team.

The first flashpoint came when the veteran defenceman Dennis Kearns, who had sat out a game, came into the dressing room afterwards and admitted that he had been hoping the team would lose. He said a defeat would have helped him get back into the lineup. I don't know what prevented me from whomping him right there. I just said that I thought he had a very bad attitude. Thinking about it now, I can see that really Kearns was being very honest and that a lot of guys thought that way. The difference between him and them is that they didn't say it. Much later, after Kearns left the club, he and I discussed all the events of this period,

130

and we agreed that we both behaved according to what we thought was right.

But at the time, I was very disturbed by Kearns's remark, because it seemed to go right to the roots of what was wrong with the team. My feeling always was that the team was the most important unit, and however much you wanted to succeed personally, you did everything you could to help that unit. In this I really saw no problem in drawing the line. It had to be an absolute thing. I never felt satisfied after the game about scoring a goal if the team lost. If you scored three goals, and the team still lost, the night was a failure. I had always seen it like that, all the way back to when I was a Bantam.

I said to my teammates, "I can't change the management's attitude; I can't change trades, can't turn the clock back. All I can do is fight like a bastard to get some success, and if we all do that, we'll all benefit." It seemed so simple to me, and I felt that with the attitude a lot of guys had, it was no surprise this team hadn't won a goddamned thing in ten years. I drove home from the rink thinking, "What the hell have I got into? This is one messed-up team." Obviously there was no tradition, there were no professional priorities on the club, and it made me wonder whether even a Sittler or a Trottier would have developed their qualities of leadership in this atmosphere.

Of course, it can be tough when you're fighting to keep your place on the team. I remembered when Toronto brought in Dan Maloney on the left wing. I said to Brenda, "Holy shit, we've got to bear down. I've got to work like never before. No going out, no visitors, no nothing. Just the old nose to the goddamned grindstone."

With Maloney I had to prove that I was worth the ice time, and I never questioned that. To me it was just the reality of a hard game.

In Vancouver, it seemed that people wanted to escape reality, have their own comfortable club with their own comfortable rules. Some players seemed to be trying to protect their jobs first, then think of the team. It was the wrong order. Sometimes one of my brothers or Brenda would say, "Why the hell do you stick your neck out like that? You're the new guy on the team. There are veterans around, guys nine or ten years with the team — let them take some responsibility." But I would tell them that I could only follow my own nature. Sittler

131

stuck his neck out, and so did people like Timmy Horton and Dave Keon. Keon had never done me any favours, but I can never deny the fact that he had a feeling for the team. I had to give the son of a bitch that. I told my family that I was committed to that tradition. My attitude might not win me too many friends within the Vancouver dressing room, but that was the way it was, and I wouldn't change my ways for any short-term popularity.

The Canucks had to battle all the way to gain a playoff spot that year, and then we lost our first two games to Buffalo in their building. In the third game, we found a better rhythm, and our momentum didn't suffer when I cracked Scotty Bowman over the head with my stick. It was an impulsive action, of course, but it wasn't without a lot of background.

Bowman certainly is a great coach, but it's no secret that a lot of players hate his guts. There's also no question that he is a terrible yapper on the bench. I had seen a lot of Bowman, heard a lot from him in my days in Toronto. We had been in the same division, which meant a lot of contact, with regular season and exhibition games. I don't know any player who thinks that a coach should mouth off on the bench. Once, Phil Esposito did it when he was an assistant coach for the New York Rangers, and I told him he should stop. He had always been a class guy — why spoil it? I think a coach, like everybody else, either has class or doesn't, and in this area, Bowman had none at all.

In this particular game in Vancouver, he was paying quite a bit of attention to our defenceman Kevin McCarthy, shouting things like, "Hey, McCarthy, they're gonna send you to the minors." Bowman started shouting at me when one of his players, Tony McKegney, gave me a hit. Bowman was leaning forward in the bench, really shouting, and I remember thinking, "You don't have to hit him, you can skate away." But I didn't. His mouth was wide open and my original idea was to push my stick right down it. But I just swung the stick. I didn't put too much weight or speed on it. Bowman turned his head, and I caught him a glancing blow. I would say there was about twenty-five per cent force in the hit.

No one got a clear picture of the incident, judging by a number of letters I received. Everyone seemed to have a different version. I didn't get a penalty, because the officials hadn't seen the incident. This, of course, didn't prevent league vice-president Brian O'Neill from getting on the telephone and suspending me at a distance of two thousand miles.

We had kept the series alive in that third game, and I believed the momentum had swung in our favour, but I was out of the fourth game. We lost, and it was the end of a very difficult year.

Apart from the difficulty I had settling into the team, the move to Vancouver presented other problems. I was shocked by Vancouver house prices. In Mississauga I had an excellent house, which I'd sold for $125,000. For an equivalent house in Vancouver, I had to pay twice that amount. And in Vancouver, there didn't seem to be much of a relationship with the business community. Off-ice earnings were nothing compared with those in Toronto. But there were positive things as well. I finished the season with 30 goals — 22 scored in Toronto and 8 in Vancouver — joint top scorer with Thomas Gradin; I had a high profile in the town; and we were living in a beautiful house overlooking the city and the sweep of the Pacific Ocean.

I certainly had no feelings of guilt about the Bowman incident. I had always been surprised at his behaviour on the bench, and in the playoff game he had been particularly obnoxious. He had behaved in a way that I wouldn't have tolerated in my own coach. If a coach of mine had carried on like that, I would have told him, "Look, if some guy skates over here ready to take a crack at you, I'm going to step aside. If you've got a message, give it to me, and I'll take it out on the ice." Immediately after the game, I had justified myself by noting that I didn't take a penalty, while one of the Buffalo players did, and we scored on the power play. If anything, it helped our momentum.

I was a little amused that Roger Neilson, who was then Bowman's assistant and who had come down from the poop deck to take over the bench, made a terrible fuss. When it came to changing the momentum of a game, there was nobody more ruthless than Neilson, but there he was telling the press that I had done something terrible — as though I had planned it that way.

The incident was still a talking point when hockey resumed in the fall. One opponent skated to me in an exhibition game and said, "I still hate you, you bastard, but it was great the way you got Bowman." At the time of the incident, I had said that I felt about two thousand hockey players guiding my stick. But I really have no excuses. I was at fault in the last analysis. Bowman had been behaving like a jerk, and I just thought, "Oh shit, let's give him the lumber."

I was determined to put down roots in Vancouver, and I felt that I had the background to really help the club grow. This belief had already brought me into conflict with some of the players. Then at the end of the season, we were having some drinks in a bar, and four or five of us were sitting at a table. From time to time, people would come over and ask me for my autograph. I was a little surprised that in only a few months I tended to get more recognition than some guys who had been on the team for a year or two, but there had been a lot of media attention when I arrived, and I had a big scoring year. But it also seemed that even good hockey players could be overlooked here, because in Vancouver the sports world didn't revolve around the hockey team the way it did in Toronto. The Whitecaps soccer team was very popular after just winning the Soccer Bowl in New York, and the football Lions also got a lot of attention. I used to say that we should change all that. We should send soccer back to where it belonged, in limeyland. As the people asked for my autograph, I was just signing the papers and handing them back. In Toronto I used to do it this way because some of the other guys, such as Shack and Sittler, didn't like to be bothered for autographs when they were out relaxing.

Eventually one of my Vancouver teammates said, "Hey, the way we do it here is that if someone asks one of us for an autograph, we sign it, then pass it around to the rest of the guys." I couldn't believe it.

I said maybe that was the way it was done in Vancouver, but it didn't make any sense to me. I told them it didn't matter to me whether somebody wanted my autograph, especially when I was out on a social occasion, and to my way of thinking, it didn't make much sense to give a guy an autograph if he didn't know who the hell you were.

It was a petty issue, but it seemed to sum up the differences in attitude that I had noticed, and during the summer these differences occasionally caused other pinpricks. Once, on the ferry to Vancouver Island where the team was going to play a ball game for charity, I told Kevin McCarthy that I wasn't very impressed with the way he was dressed. "Hey," he said, "we're doing this on our own time." I said no, it was hockey time, Vancouver Canucks time. We were professional hockey players, and we had a place in the public eye, so the club was entitled to expect us to look smart and businesslike when we went out into the community.

It was something I had been taught in Toronto. In my first year I hadn't made any effort. Once I had been invited to lunch by Bill Brown, a big man with a national wine company, and I showed up in cutoff jeans. We met at a fashionable restaurant. Brown gave me a lecture and arranged with the head waiter for us to eat at the back.

Of course, on our own, we could all find ways of relaxing, seek our own breaks, but when we travelled together we had to be aware of the kind of impact we were making. (I had had that problem with Imlach over the dress code, but that was a different matter. I had learned to accept the principle that you had to look smart. Imlach's dress code had been used as an irritant, a weapon against the team.)

Incidents like these showed that the team still had problems as I headed into my first full season with Vancouver. Chris Oddlcifson was a good captain, a good hockey player and a fine guy, but there wasn't a lot he could do about the overall situation. It was as though the club had a captive audience, and the team didn't have to do more because they were already getting good crowds. So any problems were not the team's fault. I'd never seen so much evasion of responsibility. When you boiled it down, the club had too many mediocre players, guys playing just well enough to get by — what we call passengers. There weren't enough guys who were really hungry. And then there was Bobby Schmautz.

Schmautz was an experienced player who had had a good career, but it seemed to me that he had adopted the recent Canadian attitude of "Let's bitch and we might get something." I contrasted that approach with the one I'd seen in a great player like Normie Ullman. When Ullman was thirty-seven or thirty-eight years old, he still wanted to lead; he was still up for everything, still angry if his team looked as if it wasn't interested in winning. Ullman was always prepared to lead by example.

135

In my second year in Vancouver, things couldn't have gone better for me from a personal viewpoint. I was top scorer on the team. I was voted to the all-star team. Everyone thought I'd become some kind of genius rocket scientist type of guy, because I'd learned to put the puck in the net. It was absolute bullshit, of course. I was doing the same things I had always been doing, only now I was getting plenty of ice time, lots of opportunity on the power play. And I was on a good line with Ollie Brasar and Schmautz. Schmautz was a good winger and had a hell of a shot — I picked up quite a few of his rebounds. I had no illusions about any of my success. And I knew all along that sooner or later I was going to come into serious conflict with some of my teammates.

Not surprisingly, my chief conflict came with Schmautz. On the ice, Schmautz had all of my respect. Off it, he had none. In fact, it amazed me that someone with such an ability to manipulate people always used it in a way that hurt the team.

One night Kearns came into the dressing room and said, "We've got to get this team going. The players want a meeting." I said, "That's a change in attitude." Kearns told us that a meeting of players had been planned at a restaurant, between 2:00 and 4:00 P.M. I said that a meeting was a good idea, but I couldn't attend at that time. I had contracted with General Electric to make a series of appearances at stores, and one of those appearances was scheduled for that afternoon. I asked if they could change the time of the meeting, because I wanted to make my contribution to any discussion, and I didn't want anyone to feel that I wasn't interested in the way the team was going. Schmautz apparently said that it seemed to him that I was more interested in making money off the ice. If I thought anything of the team, I would cancel the deal at the store. I got mad and said I didn't need this shit. I had given my word, signed a contract, and I had to be at that store. I was willing to attend a players' meeting at any time except the one time they had set. Otherwise they could stick it in their ear.

On the following night — after the players' meeting — I got calls from about eight players. I remember particularly calls from Glen Hanlon, Colin Campbell, B. J. MacDonald and Curt Fraser. None of them seemed to know precisely what would happen at a meeting that had been arranged between the players and management, but it seemed clear that a group led by

136

Schmautz and Kearns was gunning for the assistant coach, Dave Dunn. They felt that Dunn was angling to get them off the club; no one could be sure whether his reasons were professional or personal. The guys calling me seemed to be looking for some leadership. They said they didn't want to go along with the Schmautz group; they didn't want to get involved in a goddamned mutiny. I certainly sympathized with that attitude.

I had no beef with Dunn. I'd played on the same team with him, and I'd always respected his approach to the game. And when Ronnie Ellis came to the end of his days, I didn't recall him dragging guys into a meeting to try to save his job. I certainly don't expect that whenever I reach the end of the line.

In some situations, there is a good case for banding together and saying to the management, "Look, this or that is wrong, this or that guy is killing the club, and as players we can't just stand around and let it happen without a cheep." But that was by no means the case here. What we had here was a group of guys playing politics.

Hanlon said to me on the phone, "Look, quite a few of us don't agree with all this, and somebody's got to say something." I was thinking, "Shit, the old bazooka's at my head again."

The following morning Milford, Neale and Dunn came into the dressing room to hear the views of the players. Oddleifson had left the club a while before, and McCarthy, who was very much under Schmautz's influence, was the new captain. He gave a kind of opening address, telling the management that there were some strong feelings in the dressing room and that these feelings had to be brought out in the open. Before Kearns could say his bit, I was on my feet saying, "Some of us here don't agree with what is going to be said; we never have and we never will, and we think the management should know this."

Kearns stood up and asked, "Who are these guys who agree with you?" I had told Hanlon, Campbell, MacDonald and Fraser to leave the talking to me. I would handle the situation from their point of view. There was no use all of us ripping a hole in the ship. I was already out in the open. Eventually Hanlon said, "I agree with Tiger," maybe because it looked as if I was receiving free board and lodging from Jake Milford. I had a few alternatives. I could have named the players who didn't agree with the Schmautz approach. I could have just gone along with the majority, but my conscience wouldn't let me do that. There were no issues you could get your teeth into, not like the Toronto drinking and the Olympic charity game crisis or the bloody-mindedness of Punch Imlach, not like the Richard Sorkin scam at Swift Current. It was just a case of guys protecting themselves, trying to make moves that would strengthen their own positions. And I couldn't say anything about that.

Kearns was let go towards the end of that season. He got his contract paid up and he was given a job selling ad space for the owner's radio station. Schmautz was also let go at the end of that season, and he was convinced that I'd gone to the management and tried to help ease him out of the building. I gather that both Milford and Neale told him that I was never involved, but I also gather that Schmautz remains convinced that I was behind his downfall at his last hockey club.

It's a depressing thing to know that an old teammate you liked working with thinks so badly of you. I admired Schmautz as a player. He was feisty and he had plenty of skill. I had enjoyed the benefits of being on a line with him. What happened between him and the management wasn't my business.

But it is true that Schmautz did exert a big influence on the dressing room, particularly on a guy like McCarthy. In fact, Schmautz ultimately cost McCarthy the captaincy of the club. In the summer of 1982 — when McCarthy still had the captaincy though he had missed our march to the Stanley Cup final because of a broken ankle — he had a few drinks with Schmautz at a golf tournament for Canucks old-timers. Schmautz took a few verbal shots at Milford and McCarthy showed some amusement. When Milford left the golf club, he said goodbye to all the guys and then said to McCarthy, "Kevin, I want to see you for a minute." They walked over to the car park, where Milford told McCarthy that he was no long captain. The official statement wasn't made until training camp in the fall, and McCarthy made a song and dance, saying that he was shattered and that he wanted to be traded. But he had known all summer.

Another example of Schmautz's influence on the team after the management let him go was the previous New Year's Eve party. He had organized the team party, even though he wasn't with the club. A few of the players weren't invited — guys like Campbell, B. J. MacDonald, the Europeans and me. Hanlon and Fraser were invited, but they elected to form a splinter party with the outcasts. It was the first time since I was twelve that we didn't have a full team party on New Year's Eve. Our little party in 1982 was nice enough, but it was a divisive thing. I felt a little hurt for Brenda, who likes to be warm and hospitable — I thought she deserved better than the exclusion in the wives' room after the games. I thought one of the other wives might have said, "Look, Brenda, this is something aimed at your old man." Then again, that kind of thing is really all bullshit. I never heard that you had to love your teammates to be a winner. On the New York Islanders, there are all kinds of frictions within the dressing room, I understand, but when the money is on the table, they all get their priorities right. True, in 1984 they lost their championship, when they were hurting and the Edmonton Oilers were brilliant. But the Islanders beat some good teams to get to the final, and no one could say that they didn't manage to get up for the Stanley Cup playoffs.

That New Year's Eve party was just part of the backlash of the departure of Schmautz and Kearns, and I was the one who felt that backlash most. Although my only comments to management had come in that open meeting in the dressing room, I sensed that not too many people believed me when I said that was the case. Big Harold Snepsts had a go at me one night. He said that he thought the trade for me and Butsy at the cost of Derlago and Vaive was one of the worst Vancouver had ever made. He also said that I only thought about myself, and that by staying away from that first team meeting, I had shown my true colours. I at least respected Snepsts for making those comments up front, even though I had to tell him he was talking horseshit. Not too many people in the dressing room had said openly what they thought.

The other big knock against me was that I always took my briefcase on road trips and sat up front on the team bus. Apparently some guys thought I sat at the front of the bus so I could whisper into Harry Neale's ear. I took my briefcase because I never thought that by playing cards I could get smart or make a fortune. There's a lot of dead time on the road, and I thought I should spend it wisely. I'd take along all

139

the household bills that needed attention and any business investment that had been proposed to me. I wanted to learn about business. I wanted to know what guys were talking about when they spoke of deferred payments or cap rates and terms like that. But this caused resentment on the team. I found that a little bit bewildering, because as I see it, we are going to have a lot of time to spend after we retire from hockey, and I think we all have a duty to try to prepare ourselves the best way we can.

It was strange that I got so much criticism, that so many snide comments were made on account of the briefcase, because in October 1981 the net result of that old briefcase was that I was able to save myself and quite a number of my team-mates thousands of dollars. I was sitting in my kitchen watching the budget speech from Ottawa, and suddenly I sat right up in my chair. The finance minister, Allan MacEachen, was announcing the axing of income-averaging annuities as of midnight. These annuities gave athletes and entertainers a way to soften the impact of taxation on earnings that were high but over a short term. Losing this tax write-off was like losing a good hunk of your savings. "Holy shit, they're going for our baby," I shouted to Brenda.

I went straight to the phone and called a guy I know in the business world and said, "Can you get me an annuity and get it all signed and sealed by midnight?" The guy said he could but wondered whether I had the money. I said, "No, but the bank does." Because of the three-hour time lapse from the East I was able to get the business done in time, delaying payment of a large chunk of tax. I couldn't help feeling satisfied when I thought about the way the guys were always getting at me for carrying the briefcase. Then I thought, "Oh, what the hell," and I started calling around. Some guys said, "I'll have to call my lawyer," or "Oh, I don't know about this"; one said, "I'll have to call my dad." I recall saying, "I don't believe you guys." Eventually about eight guys on the team, including the Swedes Thomas Gradin, Lars Lindgrin, Lars Molin, and Anders Elde-brink, plus Glen Hanlon, took out annuities that saved them a lot of money.

What interested me about that episode was that the only guy who said *thank you* was Hanlon, who took Brenda and me out for supper. It wasn't any big deal, but I thought it gave a little insight into some attitudes. I thought one of those other guys might have made a little gesture. Like saying *thank you.*

There always seemed to be those little irritations in Vancouver, but in my second year, the 1980–81 season, I was able to turn all the irritations off the ice into pure fuel on it. I raced to my best goals total. I got 35 goals in all and made the undiplomatic comment that the club was in trouble if I was the top scorer. I got voted to the all-star team, the first ever Vancouver Canuck. My change of status was amazing. Suddenly writers gathered around my stall in the dressing room and said things like, "Jeez, Tiger, your skating has really improved," and it was the biggest bunch of bullshit I'd ever heard. I was the same player I'd always been, but now I was getting a lot of ice time, and I was knocking in some goals, picking up rebounds. I could play a lousy game, tap in two goals and be a hero. It was kind of amusing and kind of sad. Other people besides the writers got on the bandwagon. I'd go to some cocktail party and suddenly all kinds of business and professional types would want to talk to me because I had developed this genius for hitting the net. You see, all the lawyers and bank managers who decided to take up those professions rather than play hockey for a living would have been goal scorers; they wouldn't have been muckers or pluggers — they would have been glory boys.

Down at the all-star game in Los Angeles I received a new kind of attention. I was put on a line with Mike Bossy and Wayne Gretzky, and I suppose I felt a bit humble. Before going down to L.A., I'd called Harry Neale and said, "Hey, do you think I ought to show up for that game?" We had games in the East, and I would get very little break, but Neale said, "Make the effort; it will be an interesting experience." I said I was concerned that I might get to like guys like Gretzky and Bossy, guys I was usually obliged to hate, at least professionally. Neale said, "Just go down and be the miserable son of a bitch you usually are and everything should go fine."

All I really accomplished in the all-star game was that I flattened my linemate Bossy. In that game, I felt a little bit of pressure because, let's face it, Gretzky and Bossy are not exactly your meat-and-potatoes, dump-it-in, dig-it-out hockey players. I was racing back down the ice with my eyes on the guy with the puck, and so was Bossy, and we collided, smack on.

141

Bossy went down like a buffalo with a bullet between its eyes. As I stood there, I could feel the eyes of Bill Torrey, the Islander general manager, burning a hole in the back of my neck. I looked down at Bossy and said under my breath, "Get up you son of a bitch, there are twenty million people out there, and they've just seen a Stanley Cup winner run down by this clown Williams." But there wasn't a lot I could do. Gretzky came over, and I said to him, "This will happen to you if you don't give me a goal," and he gave me kind of a half smile. Back then, Gretzky didn't say much, but you got the impression that he knew he was going to be the best. Bossy got to his feet, and I said *thank you* to God. The all-star game was mostly bullshit, but I enjoyed being around all those great players. I was amazed when Bob Daily of Philadelphia lit up a cigarette between periods. I was tempted to say something, but I thought it might be out of place, and Daily is a big guy.

It was a good thing for my career, going down to Los Angeles. Afterwards I wished I'd taken Brenda, because it was something we could have talked about when we got older. But then, what-the-hell. The all-star game is about people dressing up and playing big-time Charlies.

I'd gotten a much bigger thrill out of going back to Maple Leaf Gardens and drilling home a good goal. Better still, our team won the game. We really beat the shit out of them.

13

The first journey back to Toronto had been in the fall of 1980. Williams had eaten breakfast with Harold Ballard in the Hot Stove lounge, and while walking through Maple Leaf Gardens, he met some old friends including King Clancy. When he scored his goal — in a convincing Vancouver victory — he rode his stick down the ice in triumph, in vindication and, perhaps, in relief because of the tension he felt within the Canucks' dressing room.

He had said that the move from Toronto to Vancouver would be a beginning not an end, and on that fall night in Hogtown, there were indeed some signs that Williams's particular approach to hockey was beginning to exert some influence. Ballard, who shortly after the Williams, Butler–Vaive, Derlago trade had announced that Vancouver had been "raped," now said that upon reflection he thought possibly Toronto had lost rather more than they realized when Williams first left Maple Leaf Gardens. Clancy told Williams that he had never been in favour of his departure.

It was the kind of psychological underpinning Williams may have needed as he sought to establish himself with new and not notably welcoming teammates. It was certainly true that by the end of his second year in Vancouver he believed that there were signs of progress — such as a more competitive atmosphere in the dressing room

— despite another ritual end to the season at the hands of Buffalo. Thomas Gradin was indicating that he might blossom into a player of major stature; and the team had been tactically stimulated by the brainy ex-Olympic coach Tom Watt, who was Neale's assistant for a season before accepting the head coaching job in Winnipeg for the 1981–82 season.

Watt was replaced by Roger Neilson, who had the title "associate coach" and an assurance that he would replace Neale on the bench at the end of the 1981–82 season when Neale moved upstairs to replace Milford as general manager. Williams welcomed Neilson as an old friend, but he was aware of the possibility of a deep irony. Neilson, Williams was sure, would bring much greater cohesion to the team. He would bring defensive discipline, the basis of all consistently winning hockey. But Williams also realized exactly what a shift to a defensive emphasis would mean for him. Under Neilson, Williams might have greater job security than ever before, but he would pay a price for it. Neilson would be good for the team, but he would not necessarily be good for his friend Tiger Williams.

At the start of the 1981–82 season, with both Kearns and Schmautz gone, a lot of tension had left the dressing room by training camp. Ronnie Delorme arrived and he had a good effect on spirits, being the kind of tough, honest player that gives his teammates confidence. It was as though we all kind of said to ourselves, "We've had enough of the bullshit, we're all getting paid, so let's get on with the game of hockey." Quite a few of the guys told me they had been embarrassed by the meetings and the conflict last year, and they were glad it was all over. I said it was good to hear, because I was sure the club was going to go places. Everyone knew it was only a matter of time before Neilson took over, and I said, "When Roger takes over, this team is going to skate in a way that no one here has ever seen."

Neilson set up the training camp in 1981 and put in the practices. He made the work interesting and the guys on the team were enthusiastic. I knew that when he took over from Neale, he would have tremendous impact at first. I also knew that inevitably some players would tire of his demands, his incredible attention to detail, the relentless way he hammered home basic points. But that would be something in the future.

In the meantime, we had guys who came to play every night, guys like Colin Campbell and Curt Fraser, Darcy Rota and

144

Harold Snepsts and there was a feeling we were moving forward. The signing of the Czech players Jiri Bubla and Ivan Hlinka brought in a lot of quality and experience, and it was a hard blow for us when Bubla went down with a serous injury. We missed Bubla's hard-nosed approach, and we also missed his influence on Hlinka during games.

Hlinka was one of the strongest, most talented guys I've ever played with. His control of the puck was magnificent. He knew the game. He could absorb physical pressure. But there was a problem. Hlinka was a floater. He played when he wanted to play, and he didn't really give a damn about the team. He once said that the Stanley Cup didn't matter to him; he had played in World Cups and that was what big-time hockey was all about. I could have floored him. The Stanley Cup was something I'd wanted to win since I was an egg in my mother's stomach, and here was this guy dismissing it. The Canucks should have given Hlinka a forty-game contract. You could be sure he would play in forty games — the ones in your own building.

At Christmas time that year, Hlinka did something I found unforgivable. In Los Angeles, after the pre-game warmup, he went up to trainer Larry Ashley and said, "No play tonight — bad knee." I think Ashley is the best trainer in the league, but there was nothing he could do about the situation. Hlinka, a world-class professional, said that he wasn't fit enough to play. When a player makes a statement like that, especially a player of Hlinka's status, you have to go along with him. But I was angry and suspicious. I felt Hlinka was letting everybody down.

The following night, back in Vancouver, we had a little Christmas party at Ivan Boldirev's house. After dinner I took a shiny $100 bill out of my pocket. I said to Hlinka, "I bet you this hundred bucks I could beat you in a skating race tomorrow morning." I wanted to see how he would react. In spite of his injured knee, he didn't hesitate. He got together $100, borrowing $20 bills from a couple of guys, and handed the money to Jerry Butler, who was holding my bill. At nine o'clock the next morning, we went right out on the ice and raced. Hlinka won by a good margin. I lost the money but I proved a point, at least to my own satisfaction.

I was disgusted with Hlinka, and there have been times when I've been disgusted with the idea of all the Europeans in the

NHL. Salming always impressed me, but beyond him I saw the Europeans as guys who worked on different, easier terms than North American players. No doubt some Canadian players had let their teams down the way that I believed Hlinka had let us down, but I felt that the toleration level of managements across the league would be a lot lower if the guy sloughing off was from Moose Jaw or Kirkland Lake rather than Stockholm or Prague. I made a general judgement against the Europeans: I decided they were a bunch of floaters, who just came to pick up easy money. Now I can see that the issue is more complicated.

Take, for example, lack of production in the playoffs. I think that many of the Europeans failed to produce then not because they were floating but because they just couldn't create in themselves the right momentum. All his life the Canadian knows the value of playoff hockey, knows that managements are not that concerned with regular season performance. If they suspect a guy can deliver in the playoffs, they will tolerate a lot through the winter. For the European the playoff time is an addition to the season, not something that has been at the back of his mind for eighty games.

It is also true that many of the Europeans are destroyed by the vastness of North America. They come from countries you can practically run across in a day. I think it is probably significant that the most successful Europeans in the league, Salming and Stefan Persson — and the new kid in Montreal, Naslund — operate in the East, where the travel schedules are less demanding.

The travel drains the majority of Europeans through the season, and then they get to the playoffs and find that suddenly they are involved in a different, faster, tougher game. Those Canadian guys they think are incapable of skating properly are suddenly a new proposition. The Canadians are guys who know that in the playoffs they can suddenly become somebodies, and all their lives they have been waiting for a chance. When the Europeans become professionals, they seem to believe that they have already arrived, that they don't have that much to prove. In the spring, a Bryan Trottier pulls up his socks, believes that he is back at day one of his pro career. A Kent Neilson or a Haken Loob or an Ivan Hlinka can't get on that train of thought, because Europeans have alternatives. They can return to their own countries, where they are already proven stars. The Canadian pro always knows that he has one shot, and it's the NHL.

That last point came to me very strongly at the end of the 1983–84 season when I had an argument and nearly fought with my Vancouver teammate Lars Molin during a team party. Molin was taking advantage of an offer to return to his old club in Sweden. He didn't think he would make the Vancouver team in the next training camp. He had some critical comments to make about the club, and when I challenged him, he said, "Do it on the ice, Williams." He seemed very smug to me. He had the kind of alternatives very rarely open to a Canadian player, so he could just walk away. Maybe I felt some of the pressures of a difficult season as I started towards him. Fortunately some of the guys got between us.

It's a pity Molin's North American career ended that way, because back in the spring of '82 he had played so well. But then we all played well. We played in a way coaches dream about and players always hope they will achieve at some point in their careers. We played well all the way to the Stanley Cup finals.

Harry Neale would probably admit that as a technical coach he doesn't compare with Roger Neilson, but he has something Neilson often lacks. Neale has the ability to whip up players' emotions, and this was his achievement as we battled strongly for second place in the Smythe Division. Neale went into the crowd in Quebec City and fought with a fan. It was a typical Neale reaction. The flashpoint came when I got involved in a wrestling match with Peter Stastny, and a fan reached over the glass and took a poke at me. Neale went after the fan, and he was followed by Doug Halward and our backup goaltender, Rick Heinz. Neale was suspended by the league, but he had left the team in a perfect frame of mind. An incident like that unifies a team dramatically, and in our case we had already established a good rhythm and understanding. It meant that Neale was able to hand us over to a coach who knew exactly how to exploit the strengths of a team that was in the mood to play.

Because I'd worked with Roger Neilson before, it was no great surprise to me that he could organize so well, hand down game plans that were like a set of military instructions. That's

147

what he'd done with the Leafs, especially in that series against the Islanders. For the other guys it was a revelation, and they responded tremendously.

Neilson's influence on the club forced me to make an adjustment. When he took over as coach, I had to adjust that much more. I had to get back to the old checking role, to remind myself of some principles I had accepted at a much earlier stage of my career. They were principles that had maybe got a little blurred down the years. My main principle had always been to use adversity, not let it weaken you or put you off your game.

In Vancouver that year, I had some sessions with the sports psychologist Saul Miller and found them very beneficial. They didn't provide me with many new ideas about how I should play the game, but they confirmed the value of the techniques I had accepted earlier. Miller's main point was that you should use the things that really annoy you, get them to inspire you rather than kill you off. In general, he confirmed my belief that it was most important to find a way to use adversity in your favour.

When I went to see Miller, some things were annoying me, all right. I wasn't playing the power play any more. I had to check guys like Gretzky and Bossy and McDonald and it was possible to check your guts out in a game and still come out minus-two. I've never complained about checking, because another of my beliefs is that the club pays your money and your job is to do what you're told. But the checking can wear you down, and you can get fed up when you think about how many players lose their jobs because at the end of the season a general manager looks at their statistics and then asks, "What did you do for me this year?" They don't always remember that you checked the shit out of some of the best lines in hockey. You think to yourself, "Oh I'll say to them, 'Hey, remember how I looked after McDonald?'" and then you get a flash of reality, and you think, "Are you kidding?"

I told Miller that I got angry about the lack of money for players who really put out, who battle through every game. And about the way I could slip from being a 35-goal player to a workhorse, a man who had got just 8 goals by the approach of spring. I didn't argue with any of it, and I wouldn't as long as I was a pro, but you couldn't stop it burning away deep inside.

148

In the playoffs, we faced Calgary in our first series. During the third period of the second game, I was sitting on the bench and my legs didn't feel too good. I needed to really bear down and produce some energy. I had to get the goddamned stuff from somewhere. I thought of the things Miller and I had talked about and what he said, and I also looked up to my Mum, always a good source of energy for me. I said, "Please give me something now." When the game went into overtime, I got the energy and I got the winning goal.

When I scored that goal I had an idea that I would skate off the ice and all the way home. I felt such release, such goddamned pleasure. Then guys came from everywhere and tackled me; the first one in was Lars Lindgren. At that point it was the biggest goal of our year — we were up two games to none in a best-of-five series. We had a huge advantage in the first round of the playoffs. At last we were rolling after those years of quick dismissals from the Stanley Cup playoffs.

We had built a strong momentum during our last games of the schedule and carried it into the playoffs. Now we had a real sense of team, and that spirit was shown in the first seconds of that first series. Curt Fraser stood and fought Willie Plett, and it was a typical performance from Fraser. He was a battleship of a player, and it doesn't matter how many submarines you've got, you have to have one or two good battleships, guys who will always be ready to fight if it's necessary. Fraser never went looking for trouble, but if anyone wanted it, he could give them more than enough. He won that fight — and others — with Plett, and waves went through both teams. Of course the good waves belonged to us.

But in my opinion, the two most significant factors in our run to the finals were Roger Neilson and Richard Brodeur. Neilson has never been sharper as a coach and in goal Brodeur just got hotter and hotter. It's also true that everything went right for us. If we had been able to figure it all out and draw it up on paper, we couldn't have wished for more. Los Angeles cleared Edmonton from the road, and that was a big help to us. We were able to beat the Kings without draining ourselves, and when we approached Chicago in the Campbell Conference final, we were all absolutely confident that we'd win.

When we looked at the rosters of both clubs, some of the guys felt that Chicago had better players. I said, "Yes, maybe so, but there's no damned way they're going to beat us." They might have good players, especially their centres Denis Savard, who is such a brilliant stickhandler, and Tom Lysiak, but when you looked around their club you didn't see too many players who would make the big sacrifices. Some of us wondered if some of our team, players like Gradin and Hlinka and Molin, would want the Stanley Cup enough. Would they come through?

As it turned out, they did, and that was a big factor. Hlinka missed most of the away games in the playoffs, but he did perform well in Vancouver, and Gradin and Molin had some excellent games. Another major contribution came from our fans. They had such impact that it was as though they called a penalty and scored a goal every period of every game. They were really great.

Two incidents in Chicago made us unbeatable against the Black Hawks: Neilson's raising of the white towel in the second game, and Ronnie Delorme's fight with Paul Mulvey in the fifth. Neilson's decision to raise a white towel from our bench in that game was a brilliant psychological move, one of the best I've ever seen in professional sport. It was provoked by referee Bob Myers. Once again Myers had come to the rink with the idea that all the fans in the stadium, plus about twenty million people watching on TV, were more interested in seeing him referee than the players play. In the third period, Myers made some decisions that we thought were incredible. He was drawing attention to himself by making cheap calls. They were hurting us beyond the specific penalties.

I was sitting near Neilson and I pointed to the stick rack and said, "Let's throw every frigging stick on the ice," and he said, "No, I already did that one time. Let's surrender." Then he raised the white towel.

Gerry Minor, another prairie boy, and I grabbed some towels and joined in and the whole situation just ignited. The photographs went all over North America, and a lot of people decided that Neilson must be pretty near a damned genius. I said to some of the guys, "Didn't I tell you he was a pretty smart guy."

Neilson's gesture united us. We were like one man — one very determined man. We won both games in Vancouver and returned to Chicago for the fifth game. That's when Ronnie

Delorme did his thing. Paul Mulvey hit Lars Lindgren with a cheap shot, and Delorme went after Mulvey and pounded him with authority. If the Black Hawks had any doubts about how determined we were, those doubts disappeared when Delorme, who is one of the most genuine men in hockey, went to work. The fight, right in their own building, hurt Chicago as badly as anything could. They were already down 3–1 in the series, and they just lost the will to fight on.

There isn't much to say about the series against the Islanders. They just had too many good players and too much going for them. But they started slowly and needed a lot of help from Billy Smith, especially in the first game, which we should have won.

One problem that bothered me on Long Island was the poor hotel accommodation. We stayed in a place you wouldn't have wanted to use on a remote stretch of the Trans-Canada highway. We had to spend half the day travelling to and from practice. The Stanley Cup is supposed to be the highlight of an NHL player's career, so it's frustrating to find that there are no decent hotels available to the visiting team, because of the demand for space from the media and league officials and fans.

But then, it was very satisfying to walk along the beach at Oyster Bay, a place inhabited by some of the fattest cats on the Eastern seaboard of the United States, and think of how far we had been able to travel. The New York papers might say we were lucky and call us "grizzly bears" from the West; they might talk about our clutch-and-grab techniques, but then, who the hell knows anything about hockey in New York?

Across North America the Canucks were described as a bunch of pluggers and grinders. There was some truth in that, of course, but we were pluggers and grinders who were producing maximum performance under a very astute coach. We were grinders turning in some flawless games. I can't remember a bad pass apart from the one Harold Snepsts served up to Bossy in overtime of the first game with the Islanders, and that could have happened to anyone.

We were hockey players and we knew what we'd done. Guys like Ron Delorme and Jim Nill and me had come close to the very end of our dream. We'd made it all the way to the Stanley Cup final. For a Thomas Gradin or an Ivan Hlinka it might be just another chore in the fulfilling of a contract, but to guys like us it was something which filled us with pride. I said we had a lot to be proud of. We had frustrated Lanny McDonald. We had blanked Marcel Dionne's line, and we'd kept that tricky little bastard Savard off the sheet. Big Snepsts had played some of the games of his life. Brodeur had kept us alive so many times. Every goddamned player on the club had made a contribution.

When we returned from Long Island, even though we had lost the first two games, the fans showed they hadn't given up on us. At the Vancouver airport, fire engines draped in our colours came racing along the runways. When I saw that, I couldn't believe it for a few seconds. Fans sometimes say that it is impossible for a team to maintain intensity for the whole schedule, and I say, "Well, if you could cheer like that all the time, maybe we could."

After all the lean years Vancouver Canucks were on the verge of breaking through to the status of a sound contending club. All the foundations were there. Most of all there was tremendous spirit. But in several ways we blew it. We blew it tactically and we blew it in the minds and the hearts of our players. In my opinion the most damaging factor was the way the club dealt with Thomas Gradin. They created two classes — Thomas Gradin and the rest of us.

When the 1981 budget cut away the tax shelters granted to athletes, Gradin appeared to decide that he would just go through the motions on the ice. This was devastating to the team, because Gradin had so much talent, was so vital in so many aspects of the game. It was as though Thomas was simply saying, "No pay, no play." So when Harry Neale burst into the dressing room and ranted and raved after a game in Denver, I wanted to ask him, "Well, who are the floaters, who are the losers in the dressing room? You name them." Everyone knew that Thomas wasn't doing it, that he was telling the club to come to him with a new deal or forget about him as a major contributor. But Neale didn't pick out any individuals in the dressing room.

Gradin had gotten a new contract as we approached the Stanley Cup playoffs. For him, the effects of the new budget were wiped away. If it seemed wrong at the time, nobody was saying much, because we were concentrating on the playoffs. Things were going so well that just about everybody in the dressing room felt sure we would be looked after at the end of the season. So we got on with the business at hand. But then when it was all over, each of us trooped to the office of Harry Neale, who had taken over as general manager. We had hoped we might be called, but one by one we lost patience. I was one of the first to go to the office, and I got no more satisfaction than any of the others.

Neale told us that the club had a policy of not re-negotiating a current contract. I told Harry that I didn't want to re-negotiate. I just wanted more money. I felt I deserved it. What angered me and most of the other guys was that Gradin had reacted so obviously to the new tax situation. None of his teammates liked it any better, but he was the only one to get relief.

The hockey club probably thought it was saving money, but really it was doing the opposite. It now had a lot of bitter hockey players on its hands. The club's attitude was that if Gradin decided to pack his bags and go home, he would be a lot harder to replace than any other player on the club, with the possible exception of Richard Brodeur. My reaction was, "So what?" So what happens the next time a leading player holds a gun to the head of management? Do they just give him what he wants, and then tell his co-workers to go jump in the lake?

It took a lot of the guys a long time to get over the fact that the player who seemed to stop trying got a new ticket. I don't mean that anybody went out not anxious to win, but there is no doubt that something was missing in the 1982–83 season. It was as though the team was a balloon, and somebody had given it a small pinprick, and however hard you tried to fill it with air there was always leakage. Stan Smyl went to ask for a new deal, and there was a good contrast between his attitude on the ice and Gradin's. A lot of people say Smyl is a good strong player who lacks talent. Bullshit! He can play the game damned well. Smyl was a fine captain in our run to the finals: he represented so much of what you want in a pro. He didn't get a deal, and that just intensified my own feelings of bitterness. I felt that I was a guy who had worked hard all his life and never quit on anyone; and I'd been shafted along with a lot of other honest hockey players.

All this was a corrosive business, and it seemed to touch all our efforts. Those efforts were also affected by the fact that we were now trying to play a type of game that was simply beyond us over eighty games. Roger Neilson wanted us to play a hard-checking 1–0 game every time we went out, and in the regular season it just couldn't be maintained. What happens when you play that style is that opposition teams play to counter it. They keep gambling, and if you don't get a lead you're in trouble. Sooner or later the other team will pick up a bad pass and score, and then you have to open it up. You reach a point where you are just not capable of opening up at all without seeing your whole game plan go out the window.

The problems of the whole year caught up with us in the playoffs. Calgary beat us in the first round. We weren't the guys who had gone all the way to the final just twelve months earlier. Then, we had said, "Okay, they might have better players, but do they have our sacrifice level? Will they be ready to hurt as much as we are? No damned way!" In the spring of 1983, it was as though no one had the heart to ask such questions — but these are questions a winning team must always ask.

We had had our moment, our opportunity, and it had gone. The problem in hockey is that you never know how long you'll have to wait for another moment like that, or if it will ever come again at all. The trick is to seize the moment. We fumbled it.

154

14

In the end, it is not the violence of Dave Williams that is most pervasive. Or the rough, sometimes brutal humour. Or the absolute self-belief, which is a mask he occasionally allows to slip, and then, noting the slip, re-instates with a show of bravado that might have brought a blush to some old fur trapper fresh from the mountains. No, the thing about Tiger Williams that ultimately impresses a person is the level of his understanding of the world in which he operates.

In the press boxes of hockey, Williams has for some time been described as a dinosaur, which in certain respects is true. What some of his heaviest critics — and if Williams has much respect inside hockey he also has some extremely bitter detractors — seem to miss is the fact that Williams is the first to admit that had he been born as little as five years later than he was, his dreams of a professional career would have been ludicrous.

Although these introductory passages are a device for fashioning distance, in practice objectivity is difficult to maintain when assessing a life as intense and committed as that of Williams. As a man and as a hockey player, he drives all who come into contact with him in one of two directions. You are either attracted or repelled. Attracted by the extraordinary gusto, the sense of life and the determination to beat any odds it might impose. Or repelled by the nakedness of the ambition, the willingness to embrace whatever compromises he considers necessary for advancement, both on and off the ice.

Since Williams's personality does not permit one to remain on neutral ground, it is no hardship to admit that the many hours of interviews for this book have only confirmed an earlier positive impression. The impression is of an athlete willing to confront all of his challenges with a degree of honesty rare in any walk of life and particularly remarkable in a world of such heavy and obvious pressure as professional sports.

It is not a perfect honesty, of course. Sometimes, like most of us, Tiger Williams believes what he needs to believe. He proclaims that he will play until he is thirty-five years old, and you cannot shake that belief. He believes that a man can achieve anything if he works hard enough, sacrifices enough, and that there is a special joy to triumph if it has been preceded by a killing effort. For example, he tells of how he recently took his younger brother Morgan for a punishing run up through the mountain woods back of his home. Their destination was a waterfall, for Williams a special, charmed place. When his brother's breathing became short, Williams said that he should press on, because when he got to this "son of a bitch waterfall," he would think he'd arrived at the pearly gates. For Tiger Williams, the belief in such rewards is an article of faith.

Yet he is candid about the uncertainties that come to him when he thinks of life without hockey. He knows that his success does not guarantee his future. He senses, too, that while he has been playing the game, immersing himself in the great challenge, there have come changes in his life which he has yet to fully understand.

He cites as an example the confusion he felt one recent winter morning. Williams rose early to take his son, Ben, to Peewee hockey practice. Williams warmed the kitchen and prepared his son's breakfast. Ben, a talented young hockey player, told his father that he was too tired to go to practice. It was a situation which defeated the veteran hockey player. He woke up Brenda, explained that he couldn't get through to Ben the importance of attending practice, and then he took his dogs for a walk. It was raining. He walked through the rain and thought of the difference between his own boyhood and his son's. He thought of Ben's swimming pool on the heights of West Vancouver and of how the kids back in Weyburn had had to scrape the algae off the Souris River. He thought of all the days he had walked to practice, and in his memory it was always at least thirty below. Most revealingly, he thought, "What would my dad think about this?" Later at the

156

rink Williams mentioned the incident to his teammate John Garrett, who said, "Tiger, these days you can't force your kids into moulds." Williams reflected that Garrett had only daughters.

Certainly there is something of the dinosaur in Williams, both on and off the ice. He loves the solitude of the bush and admits that while he has the most expensive of hunting equipment — a magnificent collection in a strongroom of his house: guns, sleek modern rifles and Winchesters and Colts from the Old West — he often prefers to just tramp around the wilderness with his dogs Tonka, an amiable Airedale, and Magnum, a Doberman. He describes the thrill of finding an old prospector's camp in the Yukon, or maybe an Indian root cellar fashioned in the ground, which he discovered once when a coyote broke from its cover.

Indeed, it may surprise many people to learn that Tiger Williams, the most penalized player in the history of professional hockey, has spent several days excavating for arrow heads, purely as a matter of interest. And surprising or not, it is completely characteristic of the man that he should choose to devote the final chapter of his book to his reflections on the men with whom he has served, at times painfully, assessing the strengths and weaknesses of friend and foe alike.

The extent of his loyalty to family might also be surprising. He accepts responsibility for his widowed sister Ann, whose husband, David, collapsed and died after a beer league hockey game in 1983. Williams felt the loss of his brother-in-law deeply, for he had been one of the hockey player's fiercest supporters. "I always tried to do particularly well in Winnipeg," says Williams, "because that's where David lived, and I knew that if I scored a goal or won a fight there, David would say to the guys, 'Hey, that's my boy.' " Williams valued David not least because he once played for Canada's baseball team, and on a tour of Cuba pitched to President Fidel Castro. The right-wing Williams's only quibble was that he should have used a hand grenade. Williams also helps to support his brother Sid, who left his job and returned to Weyburn to train for a shot at the Canadian Olympic boxing team.

In the summer of 1984, when this book was being written, Williams was clearly heading towards a testing point, perhaps the greatest testing point of his career. The Vancouver Canucks had recently signed a new coach, Bill La Forge, who at thirty-two was Williams's senior by just two years. Agent Herb Pinder opened negotiations with the Canucks' general manager, Harry Neale. Neale was known to be an admirer of Williams's ability to generate an aggressive attitude, but the general manager would have to consider the views of his new coach. Williams,

157

superficially, was impervious to any pressure. He said that he was as strong as he was ten years earlier, when he travelled across the continent with old Torchy Schell, only now his brain worked more efficiently.

He had battled down the years and his satisfaction with the result was transparent enough. He said he had achieved all the goals he set himself as hockey player, family man and solid member of society. Even the most jaundiced observers might concede him these claims.

Most of all, they would have to allow that he had done what he said he would. He had lasted the course.

As a pro I've shared dressing rooms with 174 players. Recently I wrote down all their names, and as I did so, I made judgements according to my gut reaction to each guy as he came into my thoughts. Every so often I placed a tick against one of the names. The tick signified a floater, somebody who had let down the club or his teammates or, more usually, himself. When I started the exercise, I thought the list would be heavily ticked. In fact, when I really thought about the guys, about the hardships of the travel, the pressures of holding a place, I found the ticks didn't come at all easily.

Of the 174 players I've known close up in the trenches, I'd describe only 23 as floaters. This makes me proud to be a professional hockey player.

It makes me proud because a hockey player has to face up to hard questions nearly every day of his life. The questions have to do with his ambition and his courage and his energy, both mental and physical. There are a lot of discouragements, many occasions when there is a temptation to duck a challenge, avoid one of the hard questions. But mostly the hockey player doesn't avoid the challenge. Hockey players are mostly honest guys, and anyone who wanted to pay me a great tribute would just have to say that I was an honest guy, that I saw things as they were and that I always knew what was expected of me. But then, the challenges have always been obvious to me; I've reacted to them without hesitation because it was in my nature and my training to do so. It was as though all my life had pointed me at the conflict.

It wasn't like that for Ivan Boldirev, maybe the most gifted player of those who received my floater's tick. Boldirev has always had great talent: wonderful stickhandling, quickness and intelligence on the ice; but he has never done enough.

158

Perhaps it would have been different if his career had taken him to different places at different times. At an early, maybe formative stage of his career, he spent some time with the California Seals in Oakland, a joke franchise. That can't have been helpful to Boldirev, but no doubt it wasn't the main factor. The main factor is a guy's attitude to life, his need to prove himself, and I don't think Ivan had that need to the degree necessary in the NHL. He had his best year when he was thirty-four. All his years could have been like that.

For someone like me, who spends his whole life trying to stretch what talent he has, it is painful to see someone like Boldirev. In some players the neglect of talent makes me angry, wildly so, but I never had this reaction to Boldirev. I felt more that his problem was one of those mysterious things in life that you can't put your finger on, and that maybe the mystery was as great to Boldirev himself as to the teammates and coaches who knew that he could be producing so much more.

I had a very good year with Olie Brasar; he, Bobby Schmautz and I were a highly productive line. But Brasar got a tick because in tough situations he tended to fade from the scene, and that's something you can't shake from your mind when the good times come around. Bob Manno had excellent skating, but he never showed the right concentration. He could have been a star but, in hockey at least, he proved himself a knuckle-head. Randy Carlyle's floating was really just a stage of his career when he believed that he had proved himself. He wanted all the glory and he wanted it too quickly. He wanted it before he'd paid all his dues, and that rankled badly with me. Cowboy Flett had one good year in Philly with Bobby Clarke, but he lived on that, and he didn't seem at all concerned about putting anything back into the game.

Blaine Stoughton is one of those players who had to have a shock before he got serious about his career, and the shock came when he arrived one day in Hartford. Stoughton once said to me that winning or losing wasn't so important. What was important was being one of the stars. He said it with a smile on his face, but I believe he meant it. Stoughton was another one who was prepared to sit on his talent, who took too many things for granted.

I was always angered whenever I saw anybody in the game do this, and maybe I magnified the degree of it. That may be why, when I came to sit down and make my lists, an unexpected picture emerged — a picture of guys who mostly did their best.

The faces that dominated the picture were set in determination and covered with sweat. They were the faces of guys like Stan Smyl and "Bonerack" Burrows and my good pal Butsy. They were honest faces. And I wished for all of them what I've always wished for myself. I wished that we could all have been better and that once we might have enjoyed a perfect season. By a perfect season I mean a time when we all played well and got away without serious injury, and we all loved the coach and he loved all of us.

It would be great to split a season into eight segments of ten games and know that you weren't going to lose more than two games in any of those segments, that you were going to fly past 100 points, and that when you got to the playoffs, you'd just about be ready to die for each other. I feel lucky because I had some of that under Red Kelly and Roger Neilson in Toronto, and we had it for a time in Vancouver. I never got all of it, but I got a lot of it, and I think a guy ought to be grateful for that.

After I finished writing out the names of the players I played with, I selected two teams I would like, one from teammates and one from opposition players who have most impressed me down the years. Again the task was hard. I didn't know that I liked so many guys, and respected so many I didn't like.

Glen Hanlon would be the number one goaltender of the team of my teammates because of his heart and his passion, and because I would need the son of a bitch to tie the flies when we went fishing and to be a good companion when we went after deer or bears. Hanlon was a great teammate. He drove out to the airport when Butsy and I arrived from Toronto. He would do anything he could for anyone, and he put everything into his game. No one was more pleased than I was when he proved himself to the New York Rangers in 1984. In Vancouver they tried to bury him, and he had a bad time in St. Louis, but he was such a fighter, "Carrot," that he wouldn't stay down.

Once, at the end of a practice, I saw that Hanlon had left his helmet on top of the net. I said, "Hey Carrot, do you think I could hit it from the blueline?" Then I took a shot and hit the damned helmet, smashing it against the boards. Hanlon always took great care of his equipment, and he was outraged. Back in the dressing room, he got hold of my helmet and started jumping on it. We fought each other right there in the dressing room, which was comical, because just the other side of the door B.J. MacDonald was giving a television interview, saying what a great atmosphere there was on the team and that it had a lot to do with guys like Glen Hanlon and Tiger Williams.

My other goalie would have to be Richard Brodeur, who played so well to get Vancouver to the Stanley Cup final. But I have trouble with Brodeur and Mike Palmateer and John Garrett, because they are guys who don't put out in practice, and I can't agree with this attitude. Practice is where guys show that they are committed and while I know too much emphasis can be put on this, I still think it's important for a team to sense that everyone is putting in effort. I would take Garrett as my third goaltender, because he is a guy who takes adversity well, doesn't get jealous or uptight if he has to spend some time on the bench, and can come in and do a hell of a job. Garrett is one of those guys who strengthen a dressing room without apparently making an effort, because they have something inside them that is very genuine and doesn't have to be forced.

My defencemen would be Jim McKenny, Borje Salming, Harry Snepsts, Doug Halward, Soupy Campbell and Brian Glennie. McKenny is there because he had greatness in him, and even though he fell victim of a disease that plagues society, even though he couldn't keep the booze away, he fought so hard to keep his game intact. He might come to the rink after a night with the bottle, but he worked like a slave in practice, and sometimes he played so well you could forget that he had any kind of problem. There was something about McKenny that drew you to him, and I would want him on my club because I'd hope to change his ways. I'd know it was at least worth the effort.

Salming picked himself. Salming was a pleasure to play alongside. He is an innovator, a battler, and he will do as well for you under pressure in your own end as he will on the power play. It was reassuring just watching him lace up his skates.

Snepsts is the honest man, the conscience of a dressing room. You know that Harry will always be along, ready to play come eight o'clock. Halward is a talented player, and in the dressing room he is sharp. He keeps guys on their toes. You get yourself an ugly haircut or a tasteless suit and Halward will let you know about it. There are times when the general opinion is that Halward is an asshole. Every dressing room needs one. "Soupy" Campbell is a survivor. He never got a big contract, but he always hung on, was always smart enough to know that after the hockey, there was a long way to go. Campbell had respect for people and for property. Glennie doesn't get into the team on ability. What he had was a certain knack of delivering a check that would absolutely rock a guy. He would do this about once every ten games, but everyone remembered. These days, there isn't a guy around who can give a check like Glennie used to do.

My top line would be formed by Eddie Shack, Darryl Sittler and Lanny McDonald. When I got to play with Shack, he was in his mid-thirties and was doing most of it by memory, but you could see what he had. What he had was mostly for the fans. But fans are important. I've probably said enough about Sittler and McDonald. The only point I would want to make here is that the McDonald on my club would be the one I knew in Toronto. I can't really judge the McDonald of Calgary. A lot has changed between us since Toronto, and we probably need another year or two before we can get things into a new perspective.

Second line: Stan Smyl, Normie Ullman and Curt Fraser. Ullman was the first older guy who did much for me in a dressing room. He worked hard, always, and nothing rattled him. He taught you the importance of thinking about the game and not letting anything divert you from what needed to be done. You can be sure about Smyl. He will give it everything he has, and if things don't go right, he isn't going to put his head on his chest. He's going to keep ploughing away. Fraser doesn't announce that he is a tough guy, but everyone knows that it's extremely dangerous to mess him around. Fraser would join Hanlon and me on the fishing trips.

Third line: Dan Maloney, Jimmy Jones, and Ron Delorme. Jimmy Jones was a smart guy, and he proved it when he married a lawyer. But he gets on to my club because of his ability to check. In the '78 playoffs he and Butsy killed off thirty-one power plays, and against the Islanders he got me off the hook

162

when I took two penalties near the climax of the series. I'll never forget Jimmy Jones for that. Delorme is one of the toughest guys in the league. He'll do what you ask and he'll never complain. Roger Neilson kept him on the bench a lot in Vancouver, but the only time he ever got angry was when he suspected some guys weren't pulling their weight. We've known each other since we were seventeen-year-olds in Swift Current. We were moulded by the same guy, Stan Dunn. Danny Maloney didn't have great talent, but he had a great will, a great intensity. I don't think I've ever met anybody in the game who wanted to win more than Maloney did. He had problems when he went from Los Angeles to Detroit, problems similar to the ones I experienced on the move from Toronto to Vancouver. He hated floaters. He didn't believe in compromises, on or off the ice. He had his own philosophy, and you couldn't budge him with an elephant gun. He's my kind of guy.

Fourth line: Jerry Butler, Gary Lupul, and Greg Hubick. When I think of the tough side of hockey, the side of hockey that doesn't have much glamour, attract much ink, I think of Butler. We played together, we drove to the rink together, we got traded together. I think of Butler around contract time, because he was one of those guys who checked his guts out and then when it was over, when his particular job could be done by younger guys, fresher meat, he was told, "Thanks for everything, Jerry, now push off." He's in engineering school now, and that's a good place for him, because he had an engineer's mind. When he got a checking assignment, he didn't just go out and do the best he could. He thought about it, he analyzed it, and then went over to the coach and talked about it. He did more than was asked, and I never thought he was properly rewarded.

Greg Hubick never had enough talent to stick in the league. Vancouver had him down in Dallas as team captain because he was such a good influence on the kids. He played thirty-odd games for Toronto. He was drafted by Montreal, then traded to Toronto with Wayne Thomas for Doug Jarvis. He married a girl from my old school back in Weyburn, and they lived with us in Toronto for a little while. He was older than me and he taught me a few things. Hubick is one of those good guys who pass through hockey and don't really get noticed but the game wouldn't be worth a goddamned cent without them.

163

Gary Lupul is my centreman on this line for a variety of reasons, one of them being the fact that he is a gutsy little player. Another reason is that Lupul has always brightened my road trips with Vancouver. When I get lonely for my kids, I look at Lupul's baby face and I feel better. I christened him "Gerber" after the baby food. He's a good kid who doesn't mind being razzed.

Selecting this team was hard, because different guys affect you in different ways. When I drew up my first line-up, Ivan Boldirev was on the club because of his ability, but I knew it would never have worked, because over the course of a season or two there would just be too much conflict between us. Psychologically, we would always be too far apart. In the end, I gave myself a little loophole and created a taxi squad, which would include young players like Patrik Sundstrom, Tony Tanti, Cam Neely and Rick Lanz. They are guys who could be on the verge of great careers. The next couple of years will tell, and I'd like to have an option on their talents.

For my team I'd want good trainers. They are so important for both morale and the practical value of knowing that there are guys around who really know about injuries and who have standards in preparing equipment and other operations like that. My men would be Larry Ashley and Kenny Fleger, who do outstanding work in Vancouver, and I would also find a job for my old pal from Junior hockey, Dick Abel.

The only promise I would make for this team is that it wouldn't quit easily, nor destroy itself out of pettiness or any lack of physical and moral courage. It would always know what was required of it. There would be a good atmosphere in the dressing room, and that is always a contribution to success. The fans would have Shack, and they would have a sense that they were supporting a team that had heart and emotion and a lot of pride, and these are things that I think fans pick up more quickly than some people within the game imagine. We might not win the Stanley Cup, but at the very least, we would break a lot of hearts.

The second team I selected would conquer the world. The Russians could come to take lessons.

My goaltenders would be Billy Smith and Ken Dryden. I've had some harsh battles with Smith, and several of them have ended bitterly for me. I hate the way he gets away with things because he is a Stanley Cup winner, and I didn't like the way he shot his mouth off after conning the officials in the 1983 Stanley Cup finals against Edmonton. But then, I didn't approve of the way the Edmonton fans treated Smith in 1984. It was bush, and it was typical of Edmonton. My great team would be all about winning the big ones, so I would have to go with Smith. He is the money goaltender and also a goon, which is a little unusual and might be very helpful. Dryden was a technically fine goaltender and a first class clubhouse lawyer, and he had the papers to prove it. Most clubhouse lawyers get traded, but Dryden was too good a player. With Dryden you'd have the good, and with Smith, the bad and the ugly. You wouldn't worry about the pipes.

Defence: Rod Langway, Bobby Orr, Borje Salming, Keith Magnuson, Ray Bourque, and Larry Robinson. Langway is the best all-rounder in the league today. He can play it any way you want, and he is very sound mentally. The only guy close to him in some respects is Paul Coffey, but I wouldn't want Coffey because of his defensive weaknesses. Coffey gives up too many goals, and with the kind of offence I can muster, I don't need too many flashy defencemen. Offence looks after itself on this team. Orr helped the game tremendously; he built it up in the U.S., and it's haunting to think of what an Orr with good knees could have achieved. Even in his short career, he could have broken more records than he did, but I suspect that he held back, especially in the year when Phil Esposito took the scoring record. I don't think records ever meant too much to Bobby Orr. He loved the game, and it seemed that he just wanted to be one of the guys, another good hockey player.

Magnuson might be regarded as a surprise choice. He certainly wasn't a great player. But he had something a lot of great players lack; he had tremendous heart, a constant willingness to fight, to compete. I've described how he once pounded me and helped send me on my early trip to the minors, and from that incident onwards I always watched him closely. He was probably the most competitive defenceman I ever played against, and I'm told he's a pretty good guy off the ice. He would be welcome on my club, especially when I could pair him with somebody of Salming's quality.

It's very impressive that so soon after the loss of Orr, Boston produced another great defenceman in Bourque. Bourque carries the mail out of his own end with brilliant timing, and while he is no better than Coffey offensively, defensively he is more adequate. Robinson is a big guy, well rounded in his talents, and from my observation of him and in listening to him talk, I get the impression that he is a sound man, a guy who would be a really big plus in the dressing room. Furthermore, he's won the Cup and knows what it takes to go all the way. Heavy artillery wouldn't shake this defence.

My offence has everything you want and everything you ever dreamed about.

First line: Bobby Hull, Wayne Gretzky and Gordie Howe. Hull was charisma, was speed and light, and I admired him a lot, even though he once sold a friend of mine a yearling bull that turned out badly. Edgar May paid $430 for it, and it was the worst bull they'd ever had down on the farm. Howe broke so many records, and Hull broke quite a few, and the thing that is amazing is that between them we have Gretzky, who will break them all, and he'll do it a lot faster than anyone could have believed a few years ago. Here we are talking about three great players who absorb a lot of attention off the ice and do it with much style, which helps the game. There's one other thing I must say about this line. I never heard Howe complain on the ice, and I rarely heard Hull. Playing with Gretzky, Howe and Hull could do the wonder boy one great favour. They could teach him not to whine on the ice.

Second line: Clark Gillies, Bryan Trottier, and Terry O'Reilly. You would need nuclear warheads to play effectively against this line. I've played against Gillies since I was ten years old, and the thing you carry away from any contact with him is the knowledge of what a strong bastard he is. If you ever want to have your nose on the back of your head, Gillies is the man to see. I take a lot of pride in the fact that I taught Trottier a little bit about the game. He would have learned it anyway, but I was around at the right time, and I get a good feeling watching him play in the big ones, shrugging off injury, taking all the face-offs, just grinding the opposition down to dust. There's no way Trottier couldn't play on any team any year. In some ways O'Reilly is built along my lines. He's gotten everything out of the ability he was given.

166

He's a tough son of a bitch. I sometimes think O'Reilly would be a good guy to take bear-hunting.

Third line: Mark Messier, Darryl Sittler, Rick Middleton. Messier is the best left winger in the game today, and as a punk rocker I guess he would have certain fan appeal. My club would always be something of a mixed bag, and Messier would be my concession to the fact that times change and so do fashions. Some things will always remain the same, though, and one of them is that a good player will announce himself in any age. Messier is hard and fast, and I like his attitude. He said something that I thought was very perceptive after the Oilers took the Stanley Cup. He said the Oilers had played so well because they had learned to have fun. He was dead right. Winners have all the fun.

Sittler would get on any team I selected. He didn't have any jealousy in him, and that is very important over a long season; jealousy can destroy a club. For example, there have been a lot of problems in Minnesota in recent years, because one guy was whining about the lack of power play opportunities, another was worried that so-and-so was getting too much ink. Sittler would unify a dressing room, which was something Punch Imlach saw as a big problem when really it could have been Toronto's biggest asset — which I already mentioned, but it bears repeating.

Middleton makes the club despite the fact that I don't really approve of his style away from the rink. Middleton likes a few beers during a season, but he does so much at the rink that I'll forgive him. Like Messier, he knows how to have a good time. But, also like Messier, he knows that he is obliged to deliver when it matters. He always does, and as long as this remains the case, no one is likely to make any noise about his taking a drink or two.

Fourth line: Guy Lafleur, Jean Ratelle, and Brian Sutter. I like the style of Lafleur, the dash and the personality. I'm not crazy about the province of Quebec, but I do know how much hockey means to the people there and I understand the pressures Lafleur has had on him during his career. For ten years he has pushed aside the pressures, had a good life, and still managed to be the game's best winger until the arrival of Bossy. At centre, I found myself choosing between Jacques Lemaire and Ratelle. I admired Lemaire's professionalism, the fact that he was always driving on his team, but in the end I went for Ratelle because every team needs a player of his smoothness and class. Ratelle always looked a star to me and that is important; it helps a team's self-confidence to have a guy who really looks the part. Sutter is one of the most under-rated players in the league, and he is certainly the toughest of that family of Western Canadian boys we are always reading about. Some of his brothers get more publicity, but none play so consistently well as Brian. He's a typical, hard-nosed prairie kid, and he could always play for me.

There's no doubt that the game has changed dramatically in recent years, but there will always be a need for players of Sutter's character, and while some people say that the age of the hard man is over, they forget that by allowing twenty players on the bench rather than nineteen, the league has made provision for a designated hitter. It may be that the strong man will have to show better skating than before, that his violence will have to be more subtle, but you can't take away from a team that quality represented by a Bob Gassoff or a Dave Semenko. Those who say you can are dreamers who've never bothered to investigate the realities, or never been on a team that has just seen its toughest guy whipped.

One thing I have to do, which is a little artificial but I guess is expected, is nominate the toughest guys I've known in the league. Sometimes a guy will come up to me at a party and say, "Hey, who are the really tough guys in the league," and I have to resist the temptation to say, "Pal, where you're coming from, they're all tough."

Bob Gassoff was the toughest hockey player I've ever known. Now, Dave Semenko is the most formidable in the league, and behind him I would put Ronnie Delorme, a clean and heavy puncher. Honourable mentions have to go to Curt Fraser, Gordie Howe, Al Secord, Terry O'Reilly, Larry Playfair, Dave Schultz, Bobby Clarke — for his nastiness — and Clark Gillies. If Gillies really had the desire to hurt people, I would put him alongside Semenko, but he doesn't. He only rearranges your face if you insist.

Sometimes now I weigh the pros and cons of hockey, run the whole business back through my mind, and then I try to imagine

168

what it will be like not to play, not to go down early to the rink and sit with the trainers and do all the bullshit that you do before a game, which becomes such a big part of your life. I hope I won't be as bitter as Lars Molin or Bobby Schmautz. I hope I can walk out of the game as I walked in, confident that I'm going to something which has a future, which will lead to new and exciting prospects.

The money in hockey is great, but it can be cut off fast, with very little warning, and I've seen a lot of guys who've been shattered by the knowledge that the big cheques had stopped rolling in. So if I have any nervousness now, it's that I've learned hockey the hard way and I've learned it deeply, but my hockey background may not be worth much when I stop playing. It could be that one day I'll have to walk into a room where the guys I'm doing business with don't give a shit about hockey, and they'll be asking the old question, "What are you going to do for me today?" And they won't be asking for something simple, like checking the crap out of Mike Bossy. I'm ready for this challenge, I think I've prepared for it, but you don't know until the action starts. In hockey, you're only as good as your last shift, and I guess it's the same outside the rink.

I know and I value what hockey has done for me. I'm grateful for the guys I've known and for the places hockey has taken me. Hockey has let me travel and meet people and do things for those I want to help: my family, kids, the handicapped; and, most of all, it let me play in Maple Leaf Gardens and all the other big rinks. Hockey let me do the things I've always wanted to do since I first had dreams.

I'm one of the rare guys who has seen everything turn out the way he wanted. I would like to have been a better player, but I guess I had just as much fun doing it the way I did, the way I had to do it.

There are some problems in the game and some drawbacks to playing it, but it has given me everything, and it has made me what I am. So, of course, my feelings run deep. So deep that I'm not sure how I'll leave. There is a possibility that they'll have to attach some chains to the Zamboni, wrap the chains around my neck, and drag me off the ice.

169

Epilogue

On August 8, just before this book went to press, Tiger Williams was traded from the Vancouver Canucks to the Detroit Red Wings. The transaction followed the usual pattern: Williams was not consulted. Nor was Rob McClanhan, a former member of the U. S. Olympic team who had failed to establish himself in the NHL. McClanhan was Detroit's lightweight exchange for one of the most controversial and recognized players of the modern game. In 1983 there had been some talk of Detroit seeking Williams and using as bait the declining Danny Gare. For Williams any bitterness was buried beneath the imperatives of professional hockey.

He had been through the process before, of course. And oddly, as he made a bike run to Squamish on the morning of August 8, he had a hint of déja vu. He had sensed earlier that his time with the Maple Leafs was over, and Williams again felt that he was on the point of separation. He cut short the bike run. When he got home Brenda said that Harry Neale, general manager of the Canucks, urgently wanted to speak to him. Williams called Neale, who told him without emotion, "Tiger, I traded you to Detroit this morning."

No, it was no great surprise. I knew that Neale respected my attitude to the game, and the new coach, Bill LaForge, had already told me that he looked forward to working with me. But I knew well that Arthur Griffiths, the son of the owner, was not one of my greatest admirers, and my contract talks had apparently stopped dead at his office door. So it goes.

You peel away a hockey uniform like you'd shed an old skin. Of course there is a jolt, however well you've prepared yourself for the moment. I felt in five years I had become part of the fabric of a beautiful city. I had good friends, a circle of people I admired and who carried me beyond the day-to-day pressures and pettiness of a hockey club. I believed that I would stick with the new coaching regime — but there was the Arthur Griffiths factor. The politics of a hockey club are not difficult to read, and this last summer the signs were clear enough.

After Neale told me I was finished, I went down to the dressing room. While I was collecting the television set I had lent to our trainers, Arthur Griffiths came out of his office and said that he didn't put any value on my contribution, either on or off the ice. I told him he should go out and find a job.

One other factor came into play during my contract discussions — Neale expressed some concern about the contents of this book. He said that around the club there was a fear that I was going to attack the Griffiths family. I told Neale I had made certain criticisms of club policy — especially of the club's willingness to jump at the demands of Gradin, a player I could never respect — but that, personally, I had much reason to appreciate the generosity of the owner, Frank Griffiths. He recently gave me a gold-and-diamond Canucks ring valued at $6,500. I might dispute the old man's decision to put in charge of a hockey club a guy who didn't have the background or the instincts for the job, but it's his club and, of course, blood is thicker than water. I didn't want to get involved in any slanging match with Arthur Griffiths. After all, I'd had satisfactory dealings with people like King Clancy and Conn Smythe and I was damned if I was going to lose any sleep because of the opinions of Arthur Griffiths. I've never believed in crying over spilt milk. I told Harry Neale that in the book I'd said what I believed, and if the club had difficulty with one of their players expressing an honest opinion, well, that was the club's problem. I think that my writing of this book contributed to the club's decision to trade me.

171

I don't feel any rancour now. I'm grateful to Jimmy Devallano, the general manager of Detroit. He has given me new life. I know that if I stayed in Vancouver I would be dragged down by checking duties — you can get weary facing the Dionne line, the Gretzky line or Lanny McDonald on such a regular basis. I've been promised a less restricted role in Detroit. I will have a chance to initiate a few things.

It is good to feel enthusiasm from a man like Devallano, who knows hockey, understands the dynamics of the game. You go through your career hoping that you represent certain qualities that have a clear value. The Red Wings operate in the Joe Louis Arena, the biggest rink in the NHL. When I told Devallano that I would help him fill those seats, he said that he knew it.

What I knew was that I had to do it all over again. I had to come up with the right answer to the old question, "What are you going to do for me today?"